CHANGING WORLD

cold data for a
warming planet

David Gibson

Our amazing planet is warming up, and the effects are impossible to ignore. It is up to us humans to find out what harm we are doing and what can be done to reverse the damage. Picking up this book is a good start, so read on and you'll find out what's happening to the planet's climate

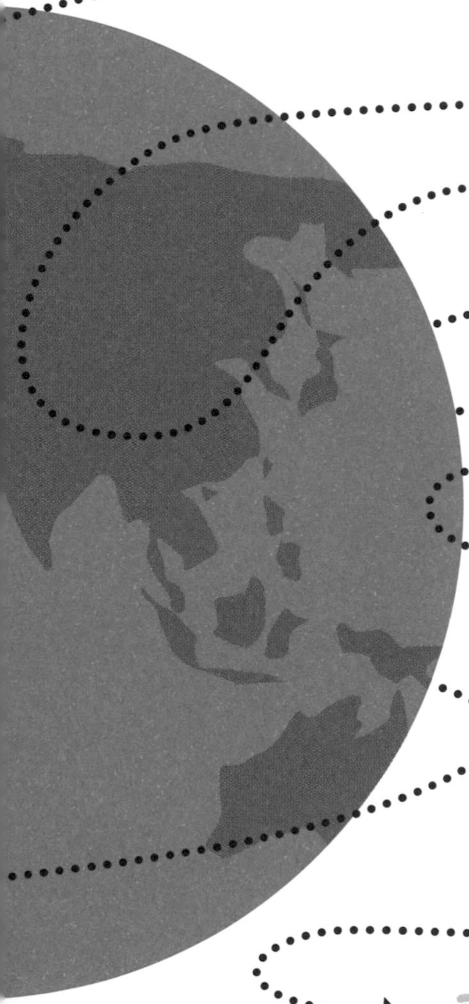

how it's affecting the oceans

and the land

and the things that live in and on them

why it's happening

and what we can do to stop it getting worse

Mercury

152 million km from the sun

Venus

Earth

Earth is the only planet known to support life

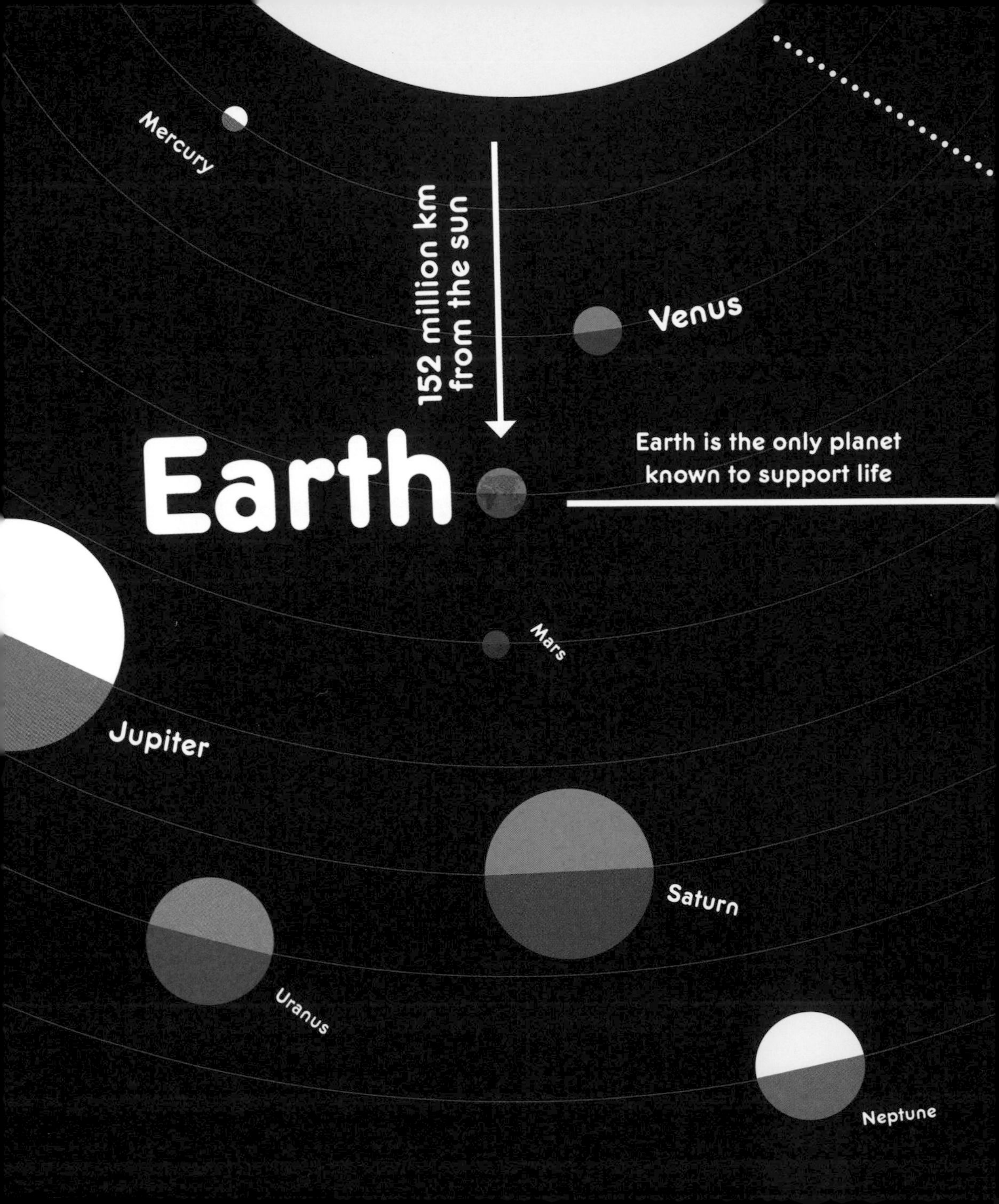

Mars

Jupiter

Saturn

Uranus

Neptune

The atmosphere protects us from ultraviolet solar radiation

THE ATMOSPHERE

78% nitrogen, 21% oxygen, 0.9% argon and 0.1% other gases

Small changes to the gases in the atmosphere can have huge effects on the planet's climate

Earth's atmosphere is like a blanket that keeps the planet not too hot and not too cold; ideal for the plants and animals that live on it

WEATHER VS CLIMATE

Weather refers to the events that happen each day in the atmosphere

Climate refers to weather conditions over a long period of time (100 years or more)

Weather can involve just one condition of the atmosphere

Climate includes all conditions of the atmosphere including temperature, wind, humidity and pressure

Weather changes over minutes, hours, days and weeks

Changes to climate can take a long time

The science of weather is called meteorology

The science of climate is called climatology

CARBON FOOTPRINTS

Fossil fuels are carbon-containing resources such as coal, oil and natural gas, which are formed over millions of years from the remains of dead organisms

When we burn fossil fuels to create energy, we release the carbon into the air in the form of CO_2

Transport

Heating & Cooling

Food

Clothing

Electrical devices

A carbon footprint is the amount of CO_2 that each person produces from all the stuff they use and consume

The average person's carbon footprint is 4.7 tonnes of CO_2 per year

HOW EARTH'S SPHERES WORK TOGETHER

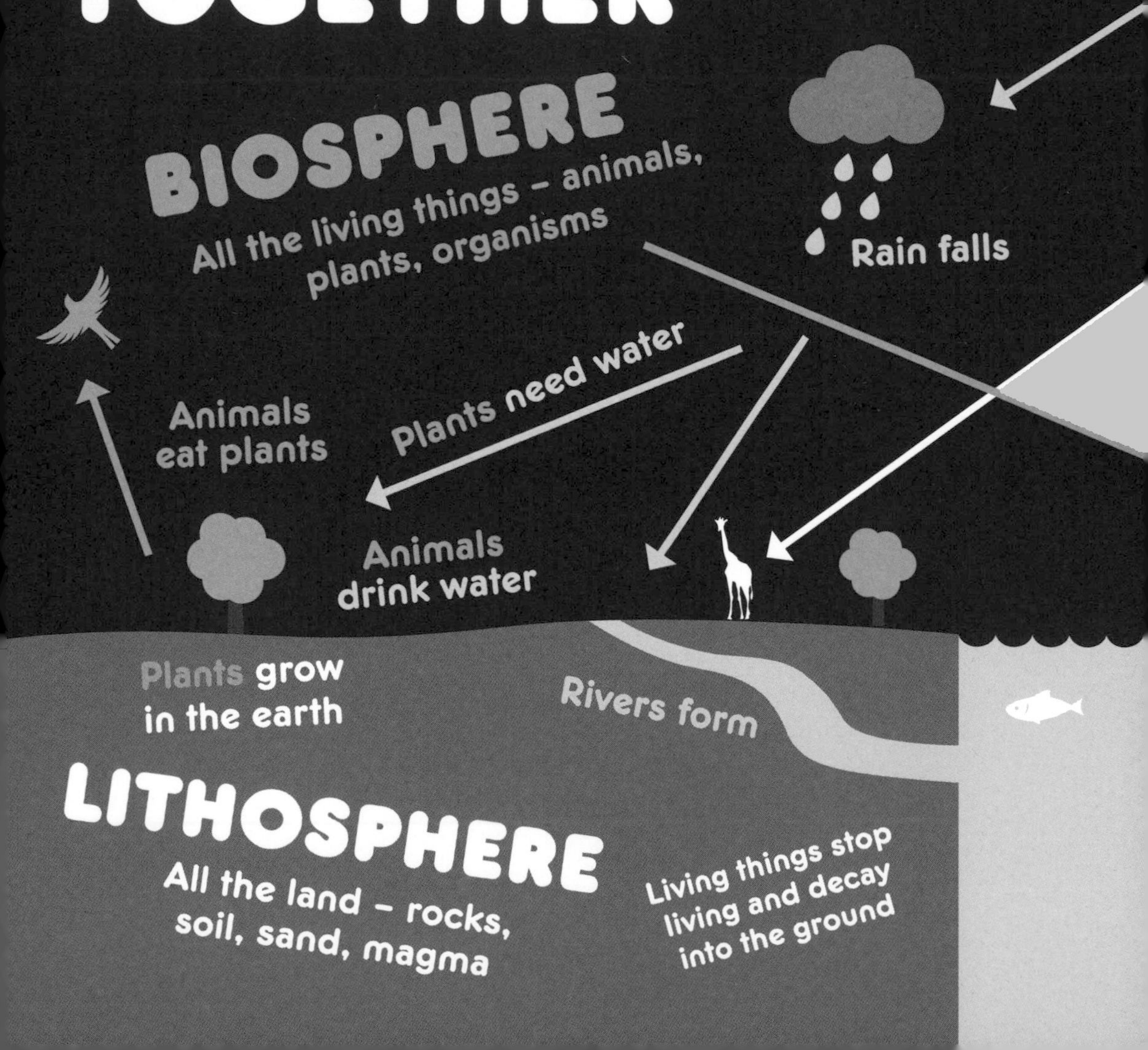

BIOSPHERE
All the living things – animals, plants, organisms

Rain falls

Animals eat plants

Plants need water

Animals drink water

Plants **grow** in the earth

Rivers form

LITHOSPHERE
All the land – rocks, soil, sand, magma

Living things stop living and decay into the ground

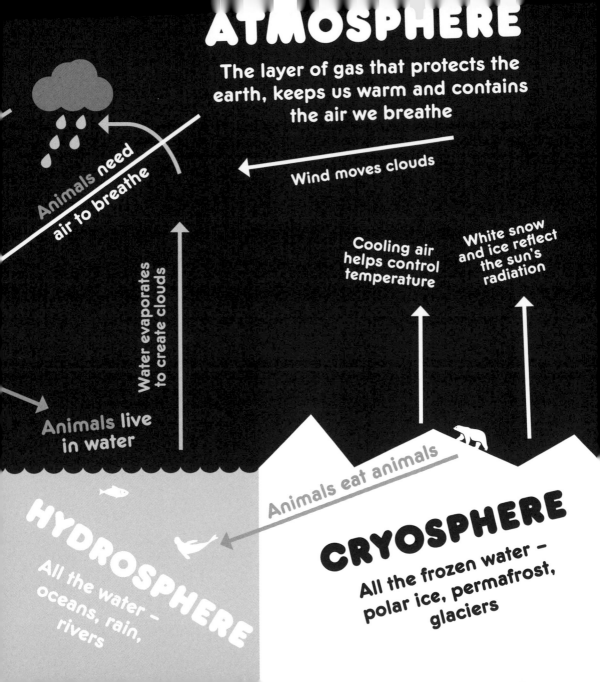

ATMOSPHERE

The layer of gas that protects the earth, keeps us warm and contains the air we breathe

Animals need air to breathe

Wind moves clouds

Cooling air helps control temperature

White snow and ice reflect the sun's radiation

Water evaporates to create clouds

Animals live in water

Animals eat animals

HYDROSPHERE

All the water – oceans, rain, rivers

CRYOSPHERE

All the frozen water – polar ice, permafrost, glaciers

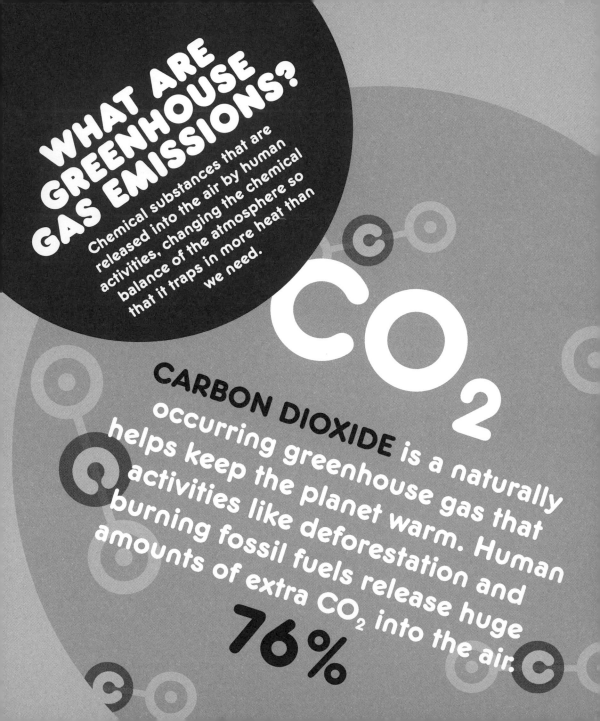

WHAT ARE GREENHOUSE GAS EMISSIONS?

Chemical substances that are released into the air by human activities, changing the chemical balance of the atmosphere so that it traps in more heat than we need.

CO_2

CARBON DIOXIDE is a naturally occurring greenhouse gas that helps keep the planet warm. Human activities like deforestation and burning fossil fuels release huge amounts of extra CO_2 into the air.

76%

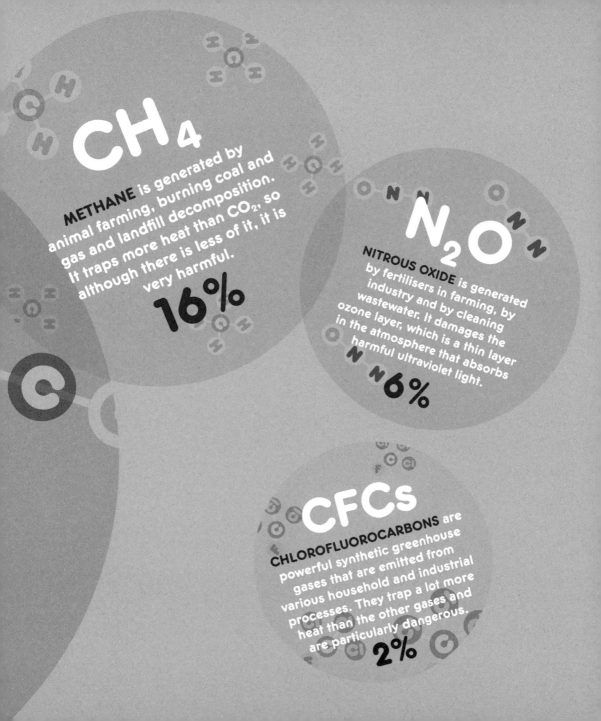

CH₄

METHANE is generated by animal farming, burning coal and gas and landfill decomposition. It traps more heat than CO_2, so although there is less of it, it is very harmful.

16%

N₂O

NITROUS OXIDE is generated by fertilisers in farming, by industry and by cleaning wastewater. It damages the ozone layer, which is a thin layer in the atmosphere that absorbs harmful ultraviolet light.

6%

CFCs

CHLOROFLUOROCARBONS are powerful synthetic greenhouse gases that are emitted from various household and industrial processes. They trap a lot more heat than the other gases and are particularly dangerous.

2%

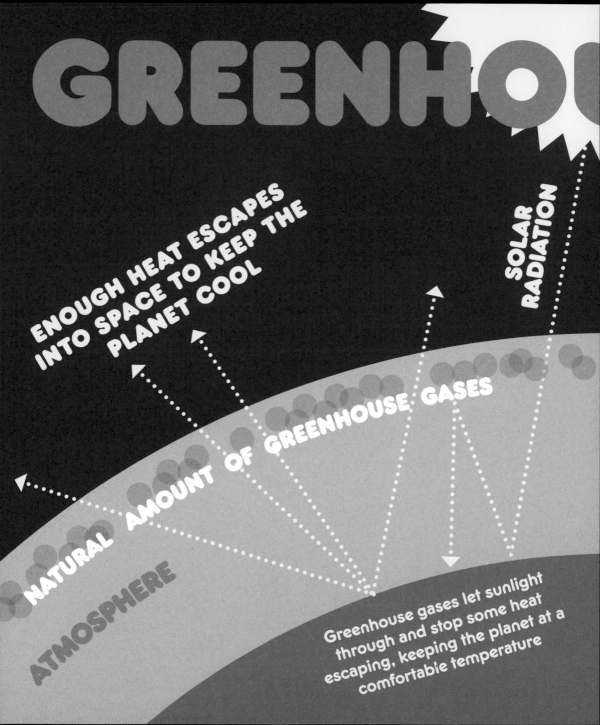

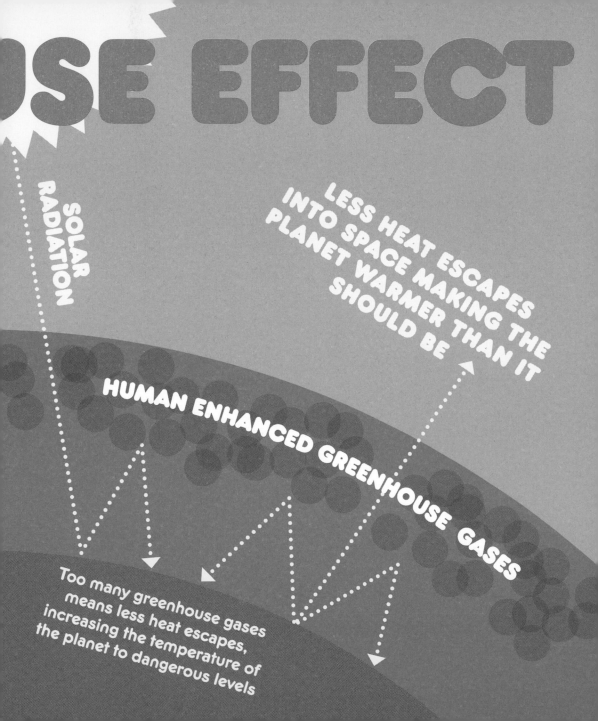

HUMAN POPULATION GROWTH, CO$_2$ EMISSIONS AND GLOBAL TEMPERATURE CHANGE 1850–2022–2100*

Global temperature is calculated by combining measurements from the air above land and the ocean surface

1850
1.2 billion people
196 million tonnes CO$_2$
0°C

1900
1.6 billion people
2 billion tonnes CO$_2$
-0.25°C

1950
2.5 billion people
6 billion tonnes CO$_2$
0.1°C

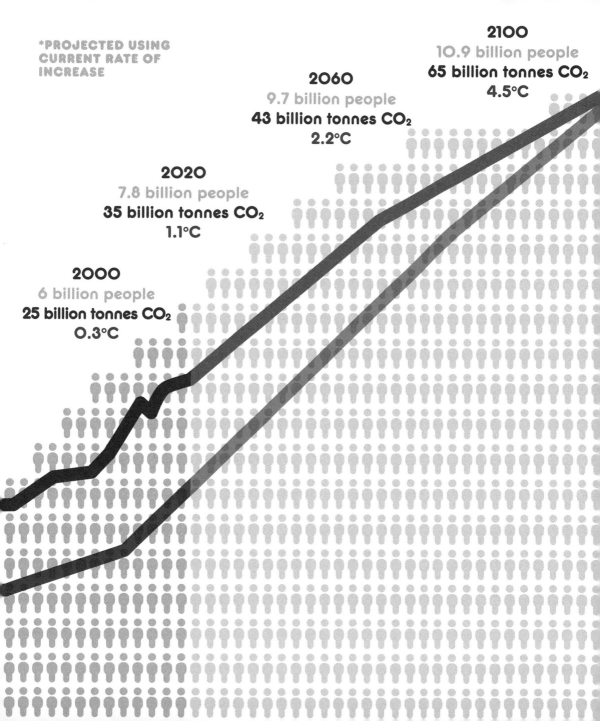

*PROJECTED USING CURRENT RATE OF INCREASE

2000
6 billion people
25 billion tonnes CO$_2$
0.3°C

2020
7.8 billion people
35 billion tonnes CO$_2$
1.1°C

2060
9.7 billion people
43 billion tonnes CO$_2$
2.2°C

2100
10.9 billion people
65 billion tonnes CO$_2$
4.5°C

IF THE WORLD HAD BEEN AROUND FOR 1 DAY...

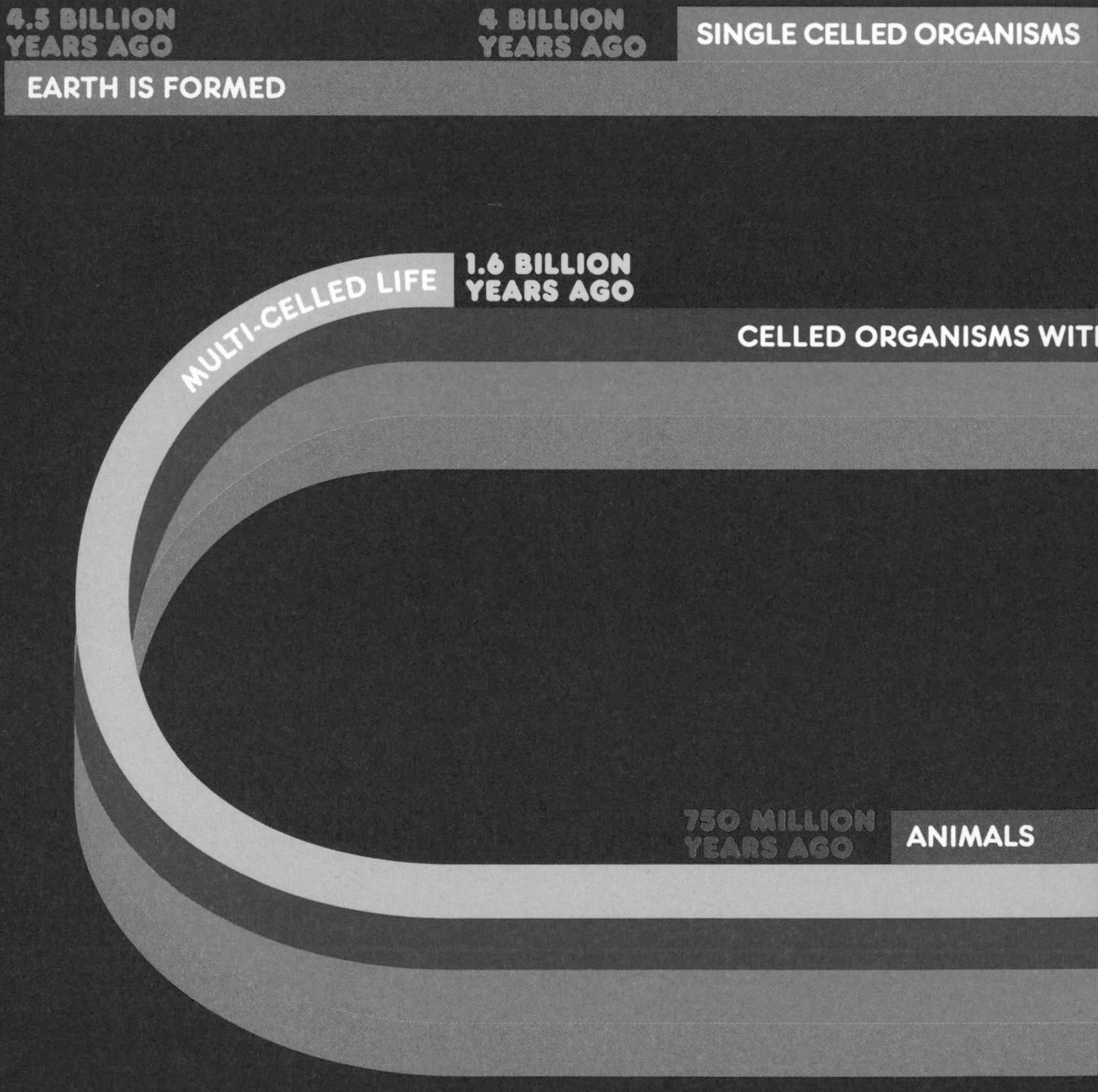

**4.5 BILLION
YEARS AGO**

**4 BILLION
YEARS AGO**

SINGLE CELLED ORGANISMS

EARTH IS FORMED

MULTI-CELLED LIFE

**1.6 BILLION
YEARS AGO**

CELLED ORGANISMS WIT

**750 MILLION
YEARS AGO**

ANIMALS

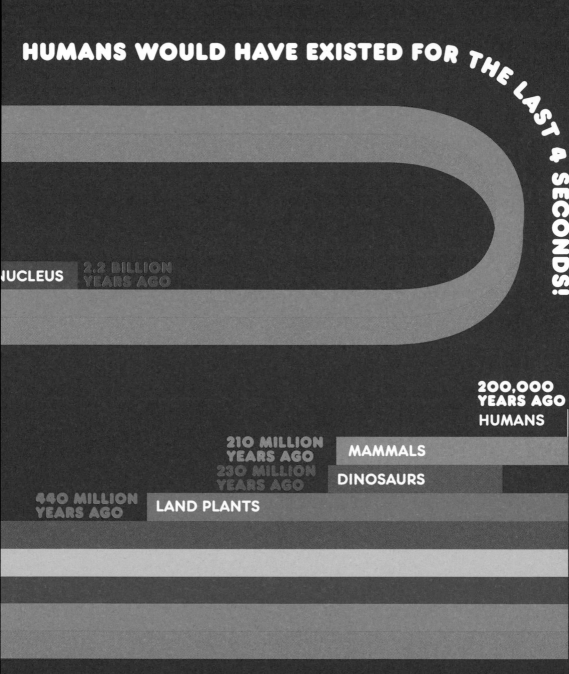

HUMANS WOULD HAVE EXISTED FOR *THE LAST 4 SECONDS!*

NUCLEUS   2.2 BILLION
           YEARS AGO

                                                    200,000
                                                    YEARS AGO

                                                    HUMANS

                      210 MILLION   MAMMALS
                      YEARS AGO
                      230 MILLION   DINOSAURS
                      YEARS AGO

440 MILLION   LAND PLANTS
YEARS AGO

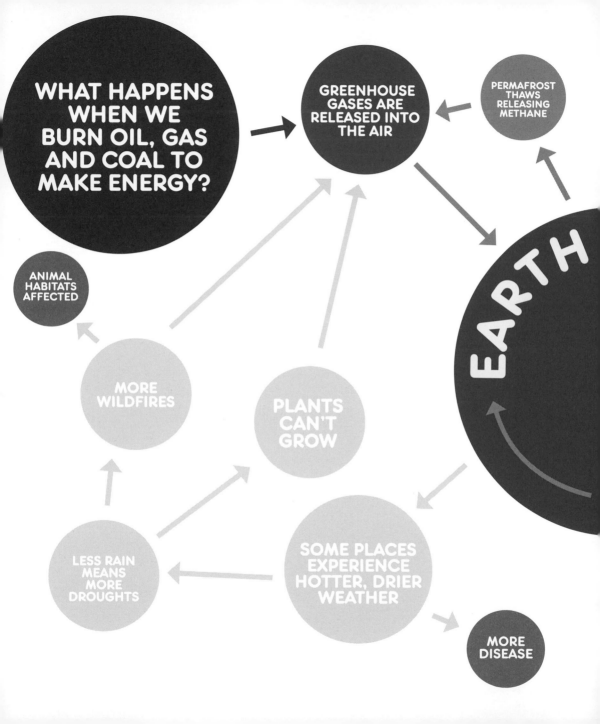

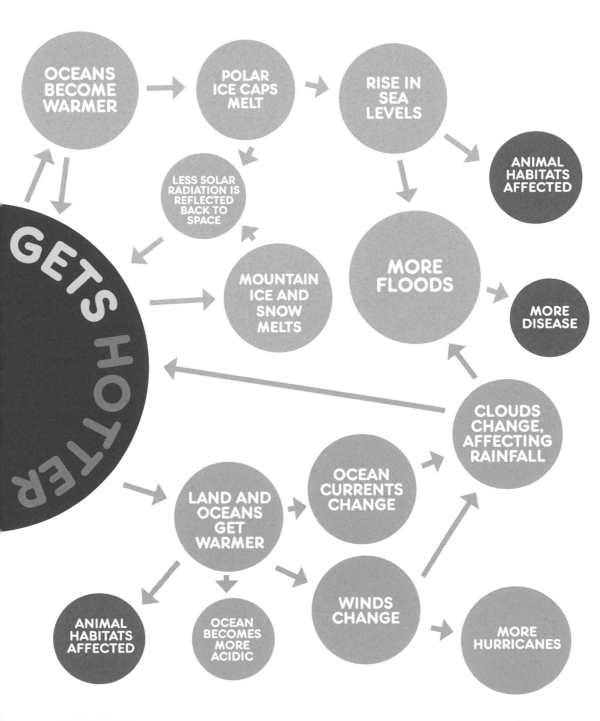

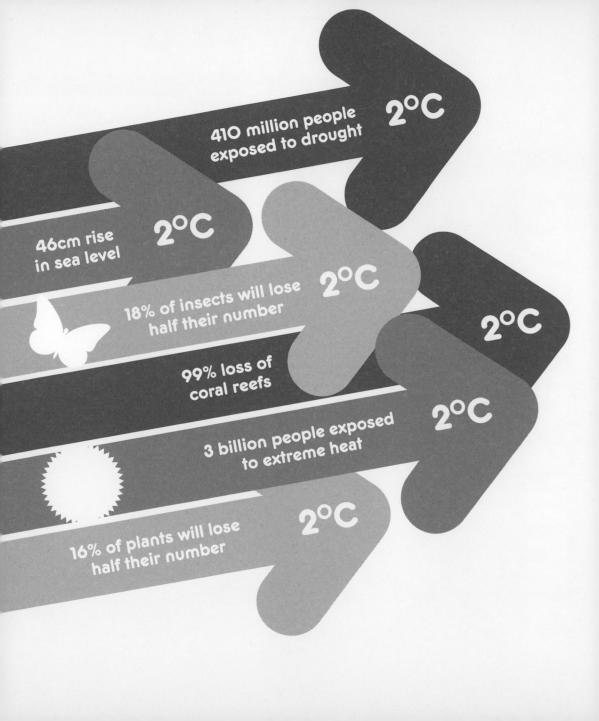

410 million people exposed to drought — 2°C

46cm rise in sea level — 2°C

18% of insects will lose half their number — 2°C

99% loss of coral reefs — 2°C

3 billion people exposed to extreme heat — 2°C

16% of plants will lose half their number — 2°C

TROPICAL

The tropics are mostly dry, with a small region around the centre of the earth where it rains a lot. The dry edges of the tropics are expanding 50 km per decade towards the poles, while the rainy area is getting smaller.

TEMPERATE

Temperate climates have warm summers and cool winters with year-round rain. Weather will become more extreme, with some temperate regions experiencing drought and others flooding.

SUBTROPICAL

Subtropical climates have hot, humid summers and mild winters. They are experiencing more extreme weather patterns like hurricanes and tornadoes, as well as the expansion of deserts.

POLAR

Polar regions are warming at twice the global average, melting the ice sheets, which leads to sea level rises and the release of methane from melting permafrost.

WH-RE DO OUR GREENHOUSE GAS EMISSIONS COME FROM?

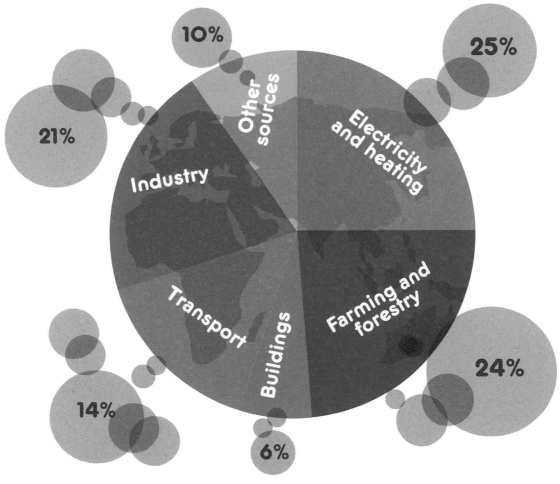

10%

25%

21%

Other sources

Electricity and heating

Industry

Farming and forestry

Transport

Buildings

24%

14%

6%

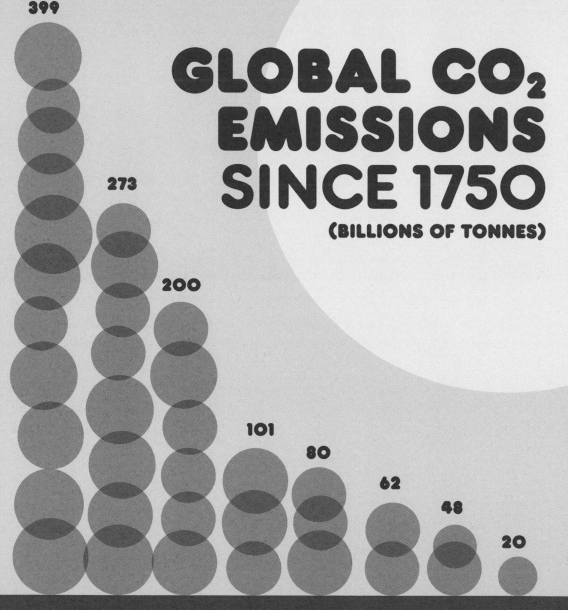

GLOBAL CO$_2$ EMISSIONS TODAY

(BILLIONS OF TONNES PER YEAR)

10.5

5.3

2.9

2.7

1.7

0.5

0.5

0.4

CHINA   USA   EU-27   INDIA   RUSSIA   BRAZIL   SOUTH
AFRICA   UK

WHAT ARE CARBON SINKS?

Carbon sinks are nature's way of absorbing CO_2

WHAT ARE CARBON SOURCES?

Carbon sources release carbon into the atmosphere

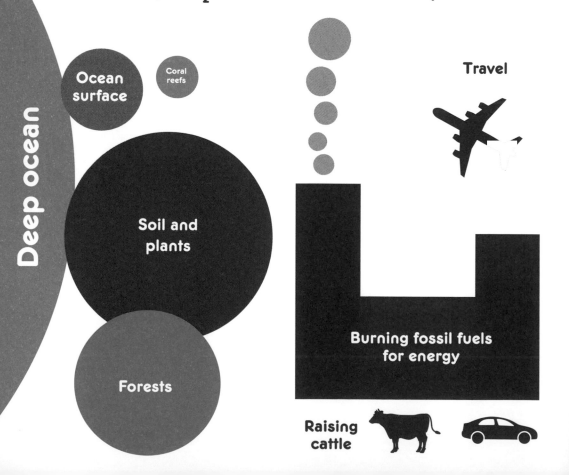

Deep ocean

Ocean surface

Coral reefs

Soil and plants

Forests

Travel

Burning fossil fuels for energy

Raising cattle

WHAT IS CARBON NEUTRAL?

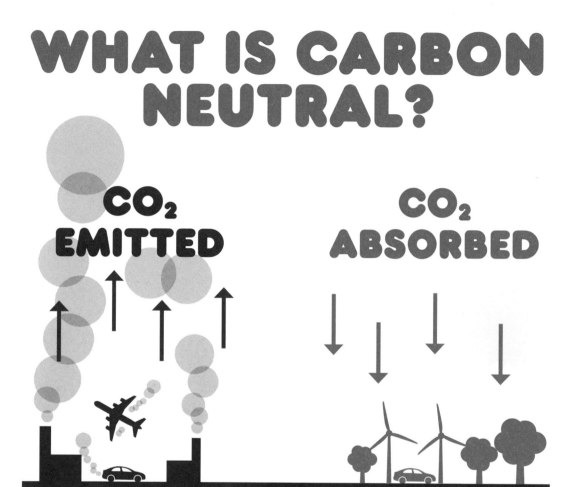

CO₂ EMITTED

CO₂ ABSORBED

A balance between the amount of carbon emmitted

and the amount of carbon reduced and stored in carbon sinks

CARBON CAPTURE

CARBON SINKS ARE BEING DEGRADED BY HUMAN ACTIVITY

SO HUMANS ARE INVENTING NEW WAYS OF CAPTURING SOME OF THE EXTRA CO_2 WE MAKE

Industries need to separate the CO_2 from the fumes they create

Then pump it deep into the ground as liquid

A leak-proof underground carbon storage tank

And we can also use those trees to make power (bioenergy)

Growing more trees and plants will also capture the extra CO_2

But that only works if we then capture the carbon and pump it underground

WHERE DOES ALL THE EXTRA CO₂ GO?

WHERE DOES ALL THE EXTRA CO_2 GO?

WHERE DOES ALL THE EXTRA HEAT GO?

ATMOSPHERE 45%

BIOSPHERE 28%

OCEAN 27%

ATMOSPHERE 2.5%

OCEAN 93%

LAND 2%

CRYOSPHERE 2.5%

HOW MUCH ARCTIC SEA ICE HAS MELTED?

FINLAND

SWEDEN

NORWAY

RUSSIA

SEPT 1984 7.2 million km²

ICELAND

UK

SEPT 2021
4.7 million km²
Arctic sea ice

GREENLAND

ALASKA
(USA)

CANADA

FRAGILE OCEANS

Oceans cover **70%** of the planet and they're getting warmer

The oceans absorb **30%** of the world's CO_2

More CO_2 makes the oceans more acidic, harming coral reefs and making it difficult for crustaceans to form shells

Coral reefs are home 25% of marine species

at the current rate of global warming, up to 90% of coral reefs will die in the next 20 years

Melting sea ice increases sea level

Hurricanes form over warm water, so become more frequent

Heat is transported from the warmer waters towards the poles

Phytoplankton are tiny plants on the surface of the ocean. They absorb huge amounts of CO_2 and turn it into oxygen. Warming oceans have decreased their numbers by 40% in 50 years

Warmer oceans are forcing fish to move to colder waters, changing the ecosystems

Fish are cold-blooded and sensitive to temperature changes. Warming oceans are causing many species to become endangered

IF SEA LEVELS KEEP RISING AT THE CURRENT RATE

DUBAI

SHANGHAI

SYDNEY

RIO DE JANEIRO

AMSTERDAM

VENICE

metres	years
LONDON	
NEW YORK 10m	700
9m	
CALCUTTA	
JAKARTA 8m	
7m	
HONOLULU	500
6m	
5m	
4m	
	300
3m	
2m	
	150
1m	
	75

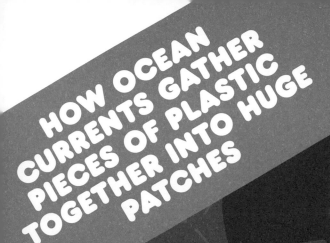

HOW OCEAN CURRENTS GATHER PIECES OF PLASTIC TOGETHER INTO HUGE PATCHES

930 billion pieces

ATLANTIC OCEAN

PACIFIC OCEAN

490 billion pieces

300 billion pieces

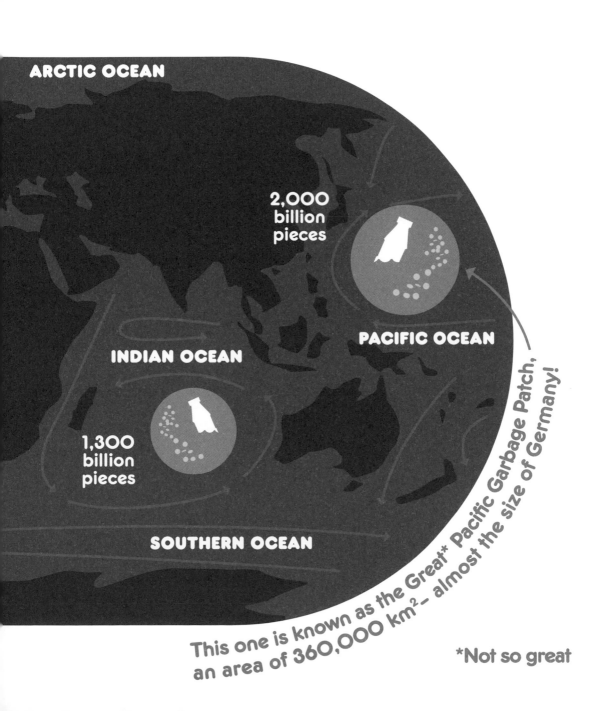

ARCTIC OCEAN

2,000
billion
pieces

PACIFIC OCEAN

INDIAN OCEAN

1,300
billion
pieces

SOUTHERN OCEAN

This one is known as the Great* Pacific Garbage Patch, an area of 360,000 km² – almost the size of Germany!

*Not so great

PLAS

PACKAGING
146M

How many millions of tonnes are made and how much is ~~wasted~~ each year?

Over 9.5 billion tonnes of plastics have been produced in the last 70 years. That is more than one tonne for each person living on Earth.

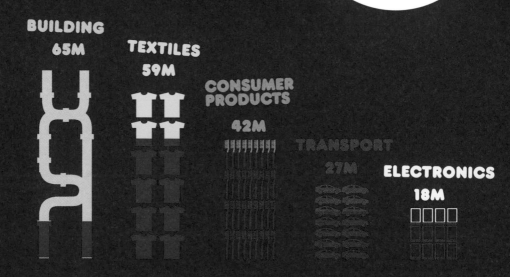

BUILDING
65M

TEXTILES
59M

CONSUMER PRODUCTS
42M

TRANSPORT
27M

ELECTRONICS
18M

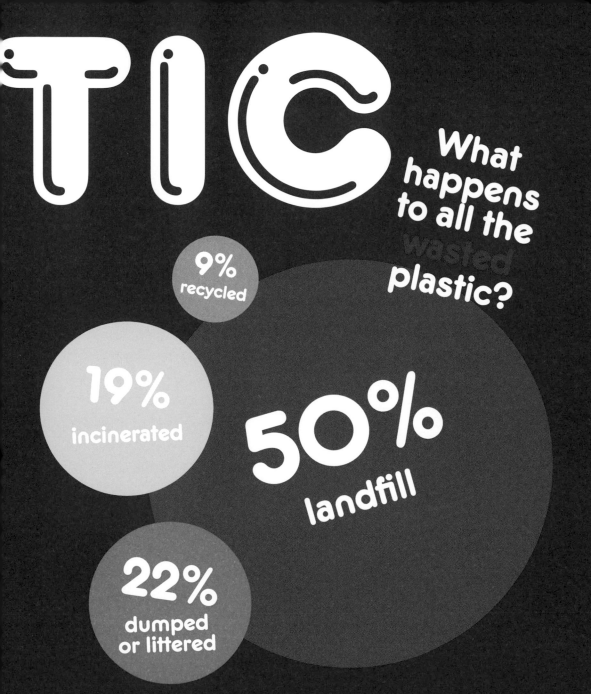

HOW PLASTIC GETS INTO THE WORLD'S OCEANS

275 MILLION TONNES OF GLOBAL PLASTIC WASTE PER YEAR

100 MILLION TONNES OF THAT IS MADE WITHIN 50KM OF THE COAST

32 MILLION TONNES OF COASTAL PLASTIC NOT DISPOSED OF PROPERLY

8 MILLION TONNES OF PLASTIC ENTERS THE OCEAN

TYPES OF PLASTIC IN THE OCEANS

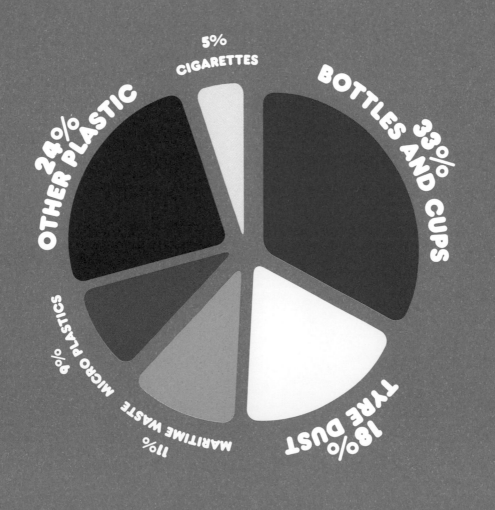

5%
CIGARETTES

BOTTLES AND CUPS 33%

OTHER PLASTIC 24%

MICRO PLASTICS 9%

MARITIME WASTE 11%

TYRE DUST 18%

HOW IS PLASTIC ENDANGERING MARINE ANIMALS?

700
species of marine animals are in danger of extinction due to plastic

100,000
marine mammals are killed by ocean plastic every year

An estimated
300,000
whales, dolphins and porpoises a year die from being entangled in discarded fishing nets

A whale was recently found with
40kg of plastic
in its stomach

Over
90%
of all seabirds
have plastic in their
stomachs

Plastic debris causes
the deaths of more than
1 million
seabirds each year

52%
of sea turtles
have eaten plastic waste

70%
of all fish
have plastic in
their stomachs

WHAT ARE CORAL REEFS AND WHY ARE THEY IMPORTANT?

THE RAINFORESTS OF THE SEA

Corals are small marine animals that form hard shells around themselves

They are home to a quarter of all marine life

Coral reefs form a barrier that protects the shores from tsunamis, waves and floods

Corals have amazing colours that come from the algae they feed off

ANIMALS USE REEFS FOR SHELTER, FOOD AND LAYING EGGS

WHAT IS HAPPENING TO THE WORLD'S CORAL REEFS?

Climate change and pollution are making the oceans warmer and more acidic

20% of coral reefs have been lost in the past 30 years

60% of coral reefs could disappear by 2030

The algae that the coral live off can't survive, so they leave

The amazing marine life that lives within the coral will die or leave the reef

CORAL BLEACHING: WITHOUT THE ALGAE, THE CORAL LOSES ITS COLOUR AND SOURCE OF FOOD AND DIES

WHAT IS PHOTOSYNTHESIS?

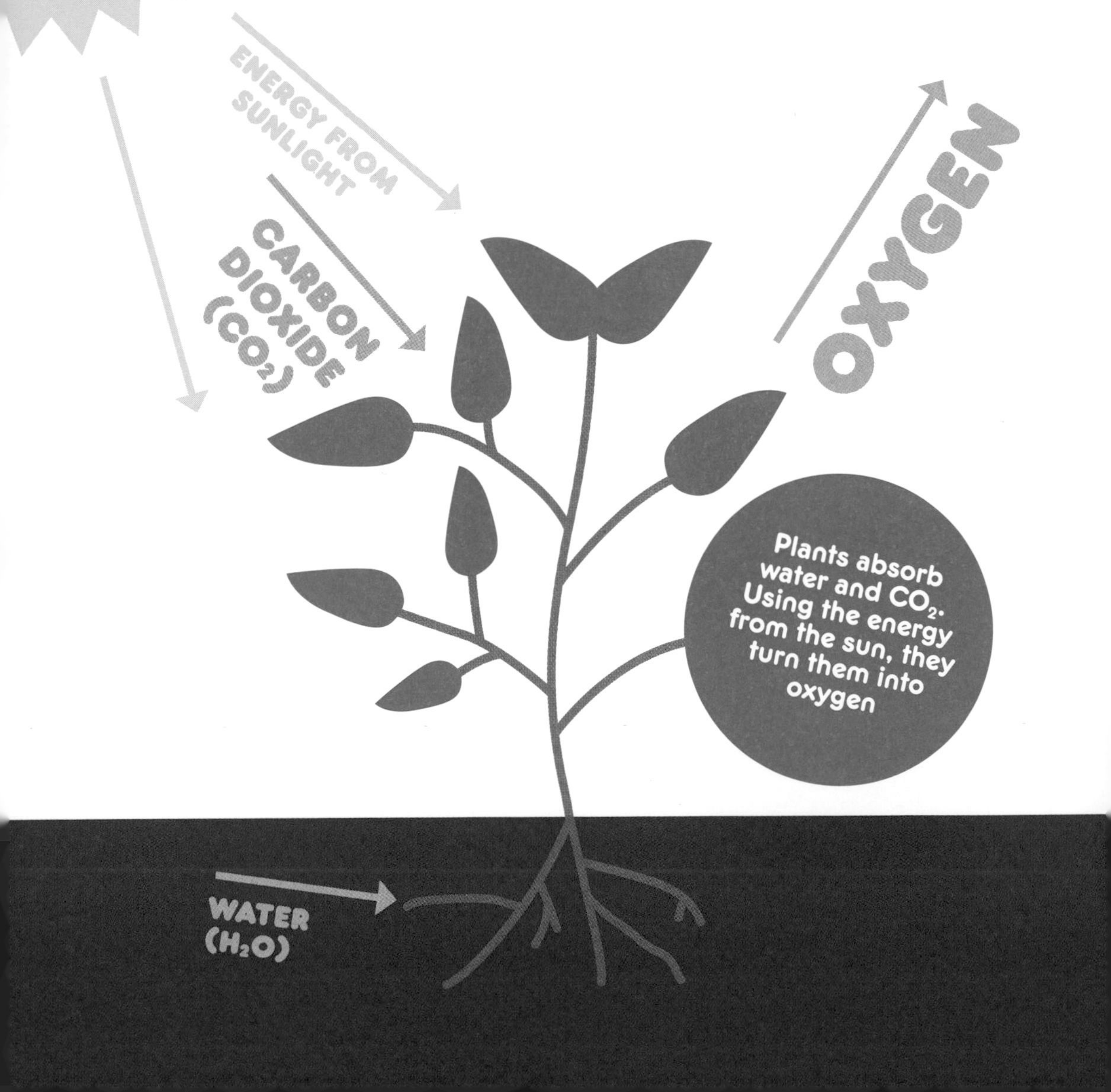

ENERGY FROM SUNLIGHT

CARBON DIOXIDE (CO_2)

OXYGEN

Plants absorb water and CO_2. Using the energy from the sun, they turn them into oxygen

WATER (H_2O)

KEEP US COOL
Trees block the sunlight and cool the air, reducing the temperature

REDUCE CO$_2$
Trees absorb and store CO$_2$ in leaves, branches and roots

FORM A BARRIER
They protect us from strong winds and rain

HABITAT FOR OTHER SPECIES
Trees are homes to animals, insects and other plants

CLEAN THE AIR
They filter out pollutants made by cars and industry

CONTROL WATER
Leaves and roots absorb water, reducing the risk of floods

WHY ARE TREES (AND OTHER PLANTS) SO IMPORTANT?

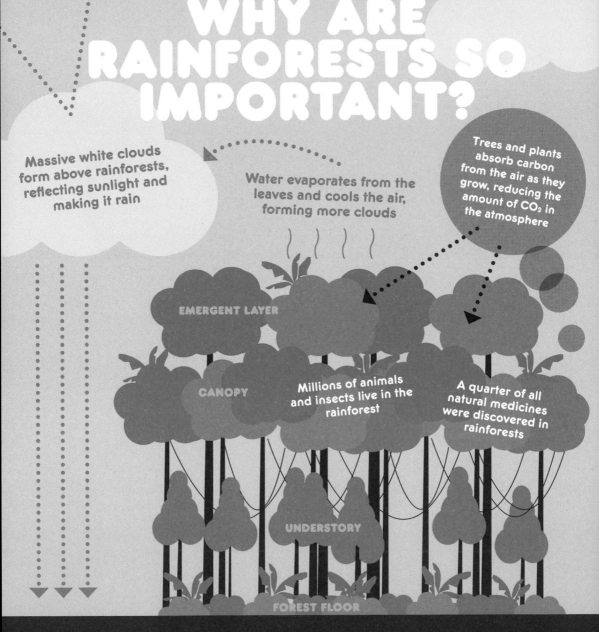

WHY ARE RAINFORESTS SO IMPORTANT?

Massive white clouds form above rainforests, reflecting sunlight and making it rain

Water evaporates from the leaves and cools the air, forming more clouds

Trees and plants absorb carbon from the air as they grow, reducing the amount of CO_2 in the atmosphere

EMERGENT LAYER

CANOPY

Millions of animals and insects live in the rainforest

A quarter of all natural medicines were discovered in rainforests

UNDERSTORY

FOREST FLOOR

Lots and lots of water is stored in the trees' roots, helping to prevent flooding

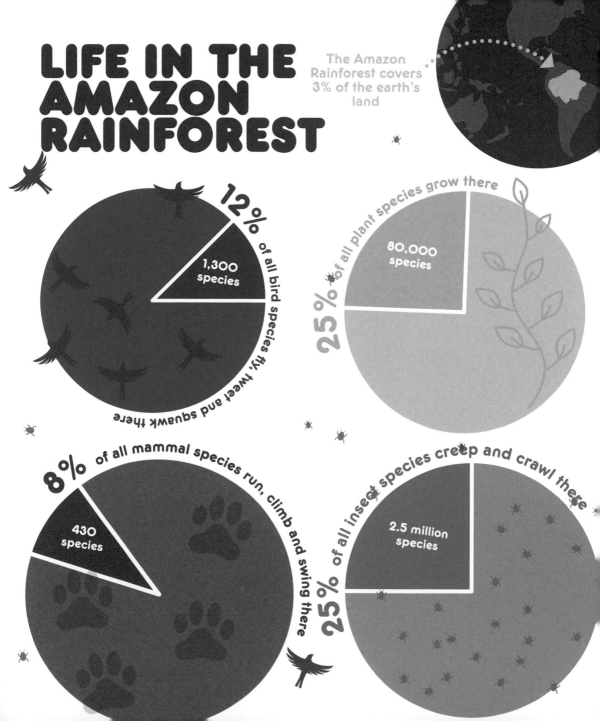

LIFE IN THE AMAZON RAINFOREST

The Amazon Rainforest covers 3% of the earth's land

12% of all bird species fly, tweet and squawk there
1,300 species

25% of all plant species grow there
80,000 species

8% of all mammal species run, climb and swing there
430 species

25% of all insect species creep and crawl there
2.5 million species

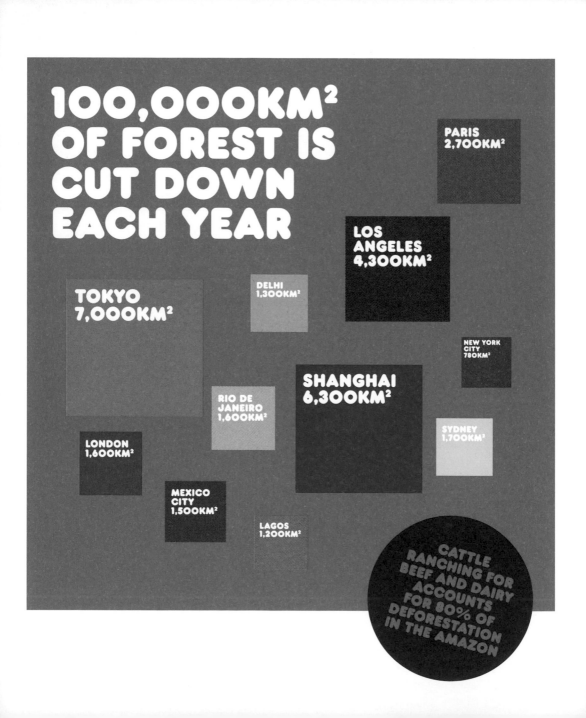

WHAT WILL HAPPEN IF RAINFORESTS KEEP BEING DESTROYED?

IF DEFORESTATION CONTINUES, THE AMAZON WILL DISAPPEAR WITHIN 100 YEARS

Less trees, less evaporation and less rain

Less trees, less water stored in roots

Less trees, less CO_2 absorbed

Loss of plant and animal habitats

Higher temperatures and more droughts

More flooding

More CO_2 in the atmosphere

Species at risk of extinction

More wild forest fires

Less biodiversity on the planet

WETLANDS
SWAMPS & MARSHES

35% of wetlands have been lost in the last 50 years due to human activity

95% of wetlands could be lost by rising sea levels brought on by climate change

When wetlands are lost, we lose an important carbon sink, and we also release all the carbon that they stored into the atmosphere.

Wetlands filter water, supplying us with fresh drinking water

Wetlands store carbon **10x faster** than rainforests

Wetlands are estimated to store over a third of the world's land based carbon

TUNDRA

Global warming has caused the permafrost temperature to rise 2°C in the last 30 years.

As permafrost thaws, the organic matter stored inside it decays, releasing CO_2 and methane into the atmosphere

PERMAFROST

Ground that remains completely frozen, most common in regions with high mountains and near the North and South Poles

25% of the land in the northern hemisphere has permafrost underneath

50% of all carbon in the ground is stored in permafrost

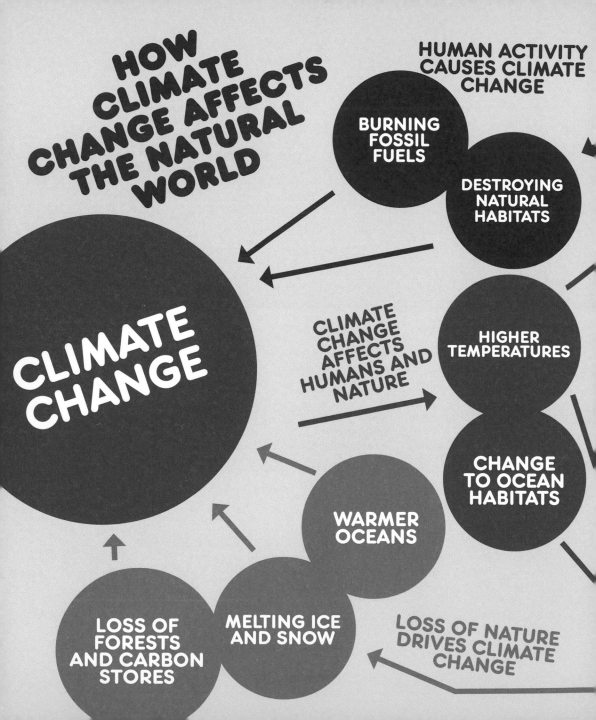

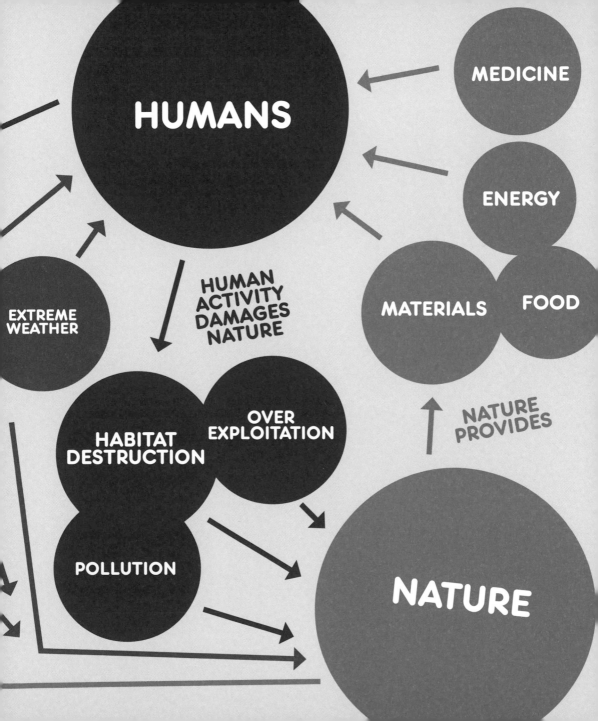

MORE HUMANS LESS ANIMALS

HUMAN POPULATION HAS INCREASED IN NUMBER BY 103%

WILD VERTEBRATE ANIMALS HAVE REDUCED IN NUMBER BY 68%

1970   2016   1970   2016

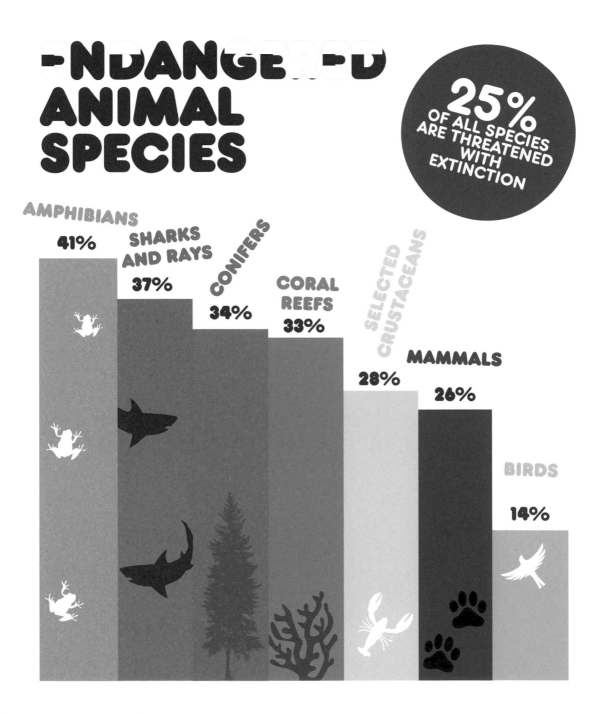

CLIMATE CHANGE AND EXTREME

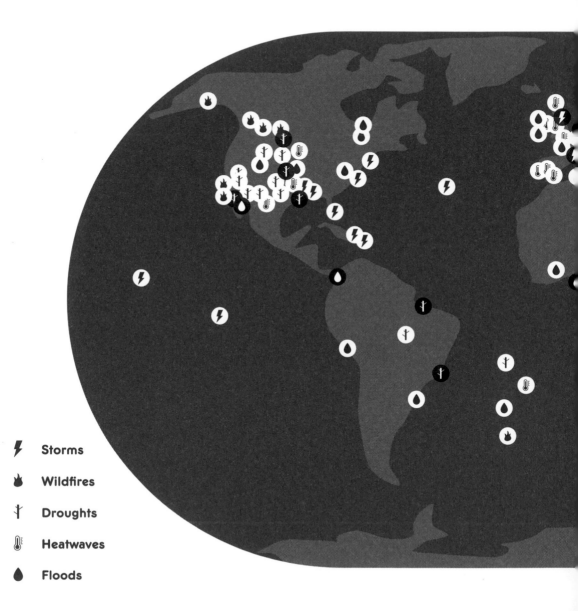

Storms

Wildfires

Droughts

Heatwaves

Floods

WEATHER EVENTS

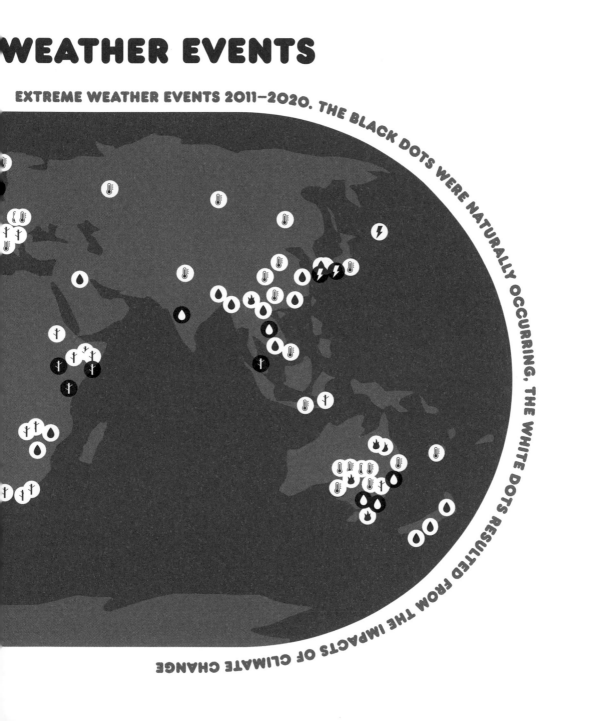

EXTREME WEATHER EVENTS 2011–2020. THE BLACK DOTS WERE NATURALLY OCCURRING, THE WHITE DOTS RESULTED FROM THE IMPACTS OF CLIMATE CHANGE

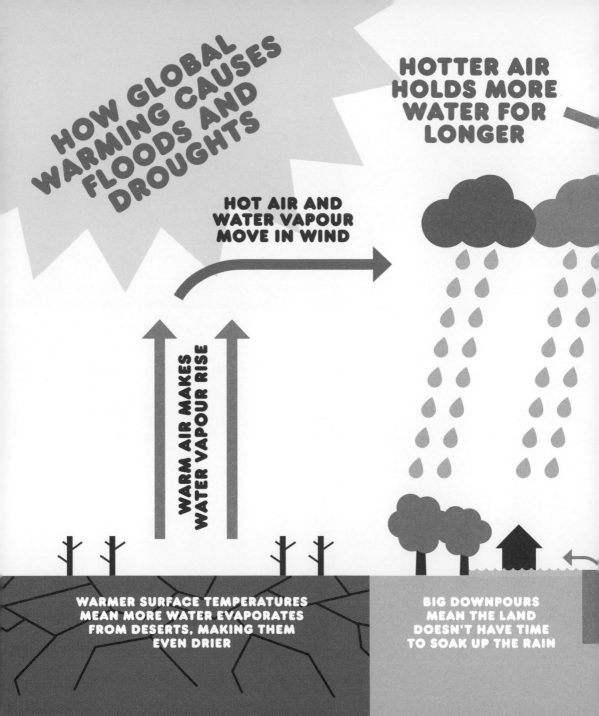

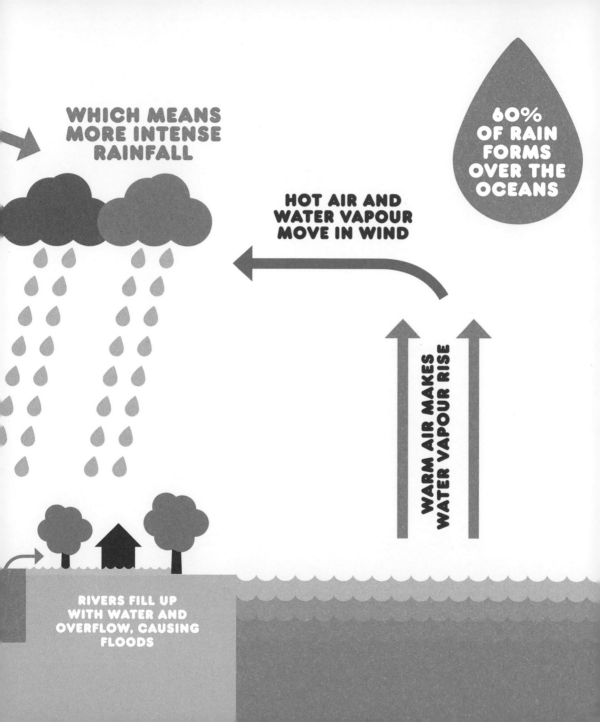

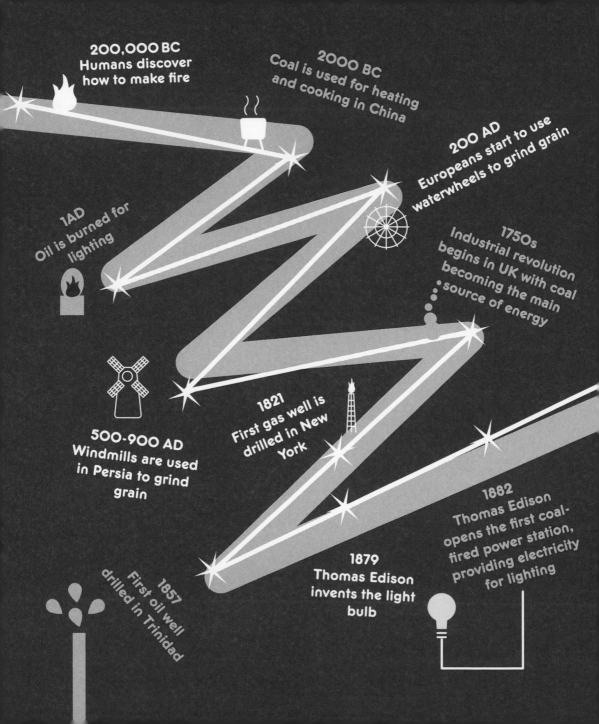

200,000 BC
Humans discover how to make fire

2000 BC
Coal is used for heating and cooking in China

200 AD
Europeans start to use waterwheels to grind grain

1AD
Oil is burned for lighting

1750s
Industrial revolution begins in UK with coal becoming the main source of energy

500-900 AD
Windmills are used in Persia to grind grain

1821
First gas well is drilled in New York

1857
First oil well drilled in Trinidad

1879
Thomas Edison invents the light bulb

1882
Thomas Edison opens the first coal-fired power station, providing electricity for lighting

A VERY BRIEF HISTORY OF ENERGY

1938
World's largest source of oil is discovered in Saudi Arabia

1950
World's first nuclear power station is built in the USSR

1980s
Scientists gather evidence that burning fossil fuels is causing catastrophic change to the earth's climate

1954
Scientists at Bell Laboratories develop the first solar panel

1978
The world's first wind farm is built

2006
Oil production reaches 70 billion barrels a day

2021
More than a hundred countries aim for net zero emissions by 2050

HOW DO FOSSIL FUELS GENERATE ENERGY?

Burning fossil fuels releases CO_2 into the atmosphere

Fossil fuels (gas, oil and coal) are extracted from the ground

The fuels are burned to heat water

The water turns to steam which then turns a big wheel (turbine)

The turbine turns a generator, which converts the movement into electricity

TONNES OF CO$_2$ EMISSIONS
FROM FOSSIL FUELS
PER PERSON PER YEAR

COAL 1.79

OIL 1.42

GAS 0.95

HOW DO RENEWABLE ENERGIES WORK?

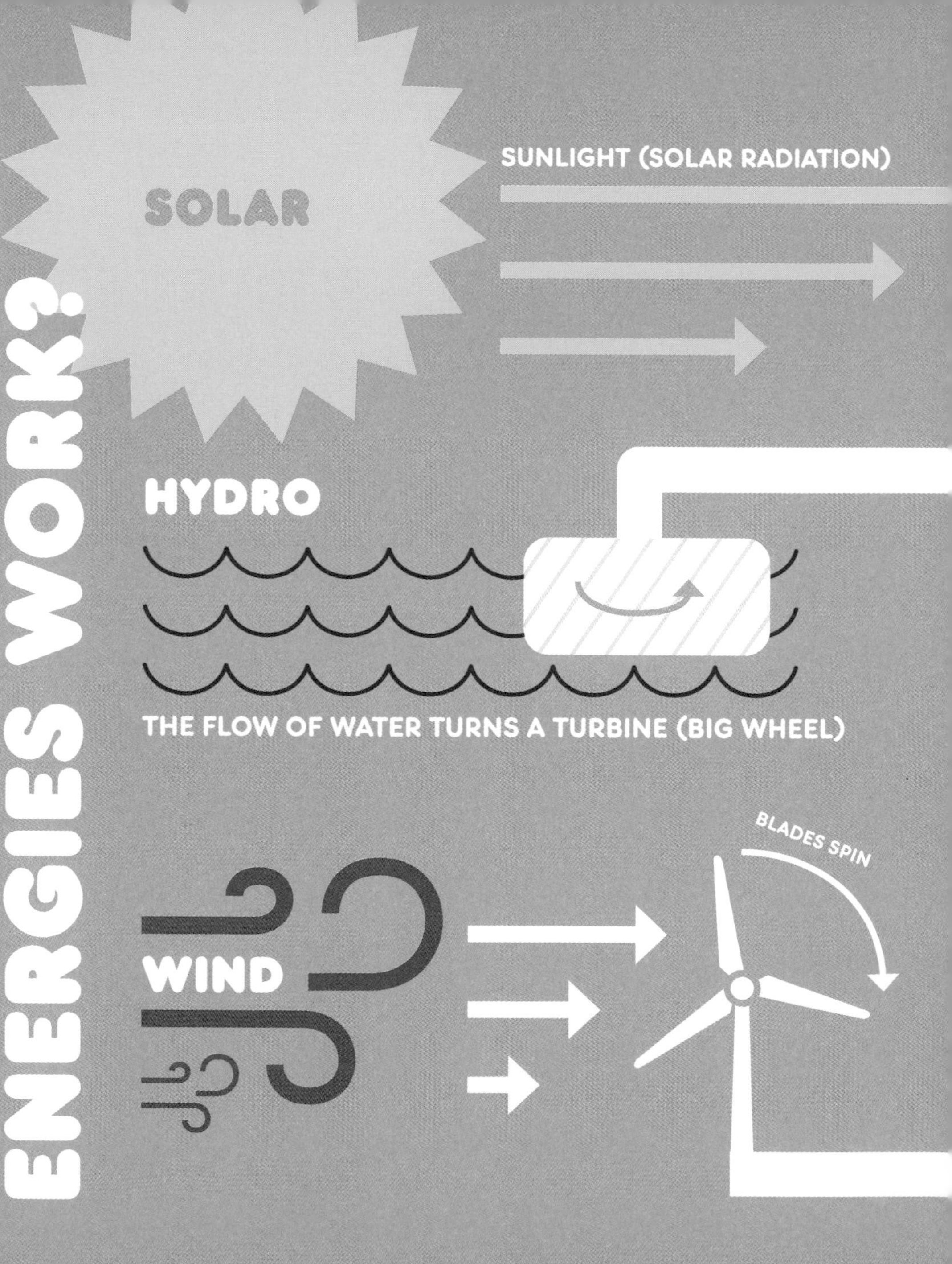

SOLAR

SUNLIGHT (SOLAR RADIATION)

HYDRO

THE FLOW OF WATER TURNS A TURBINE (BIG WHEEL)

WIND

BLADES SPIN

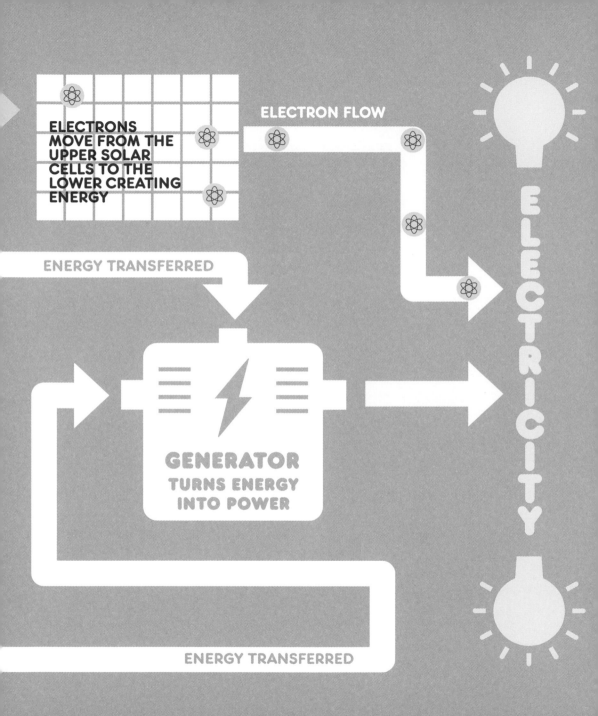

HOW GREEN ARE GREEN ENERGIES?

GRAMS OF CO² PER KILOWATT OF ELECTRICITY PRODUCED

COAL PRODUCES 1,001 GRAMS OF CO_2 — A CIRCLE ABOUT 10 TIMES THE SIZE OF THIS PAGE

GEOTHERMAL
45G CO_2

SOLAR
22G CO_2

HYDRO
20G CO_2

WIND
12G CO_2

WHO'S USING THE MOST (NOT MUCH) RENEWABLE ENERGY?

////////////////////////////////	13%	GERMANY
////////////////////////////////	12%	UK
////////////////////////////////	11%	SWEDEN
////////////////////////////////	10%	SPAIN
////////////////////////////////	9%	ITALY
////////////////////////////////	7%	BRAZIL
////////////////////////////////	5%	JAPAN
////////////////////////////////	5%	TURKEY
////////////////////////////////	5%	AUSTRALIA
////////////////////////////////	4%	USA

THE CARBON COST OF TRANSPORT

CO₂ EMISSIONS PER PASSENGER PER KM

FLIGHT 255g

PETROL CAR (1 passenger) 190g

PETROL CAR (2 passengers) 95g

 TRAIN 40g

 BUS 38g

 BICYCLE 0g / NONE / ZERO

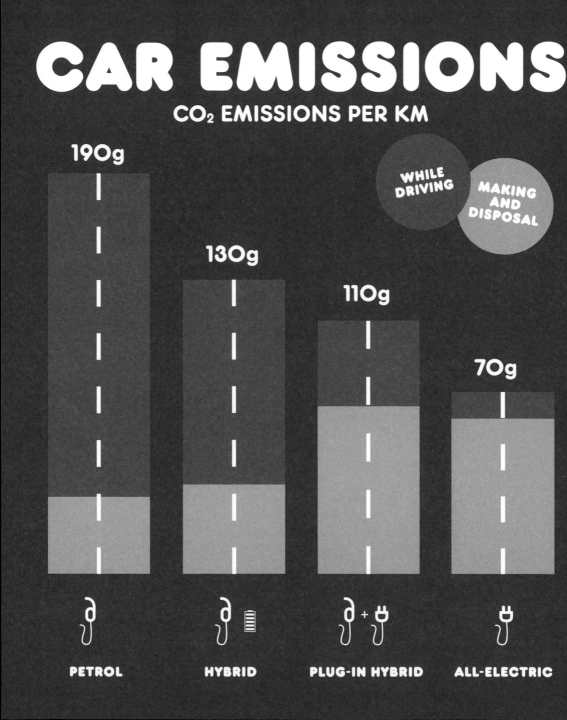

WHO HAS THE BIGGEST TRAVEL CARBON FOOTPRINT?

CO_2 EMISSIONS PER PERSON IN TONNES*

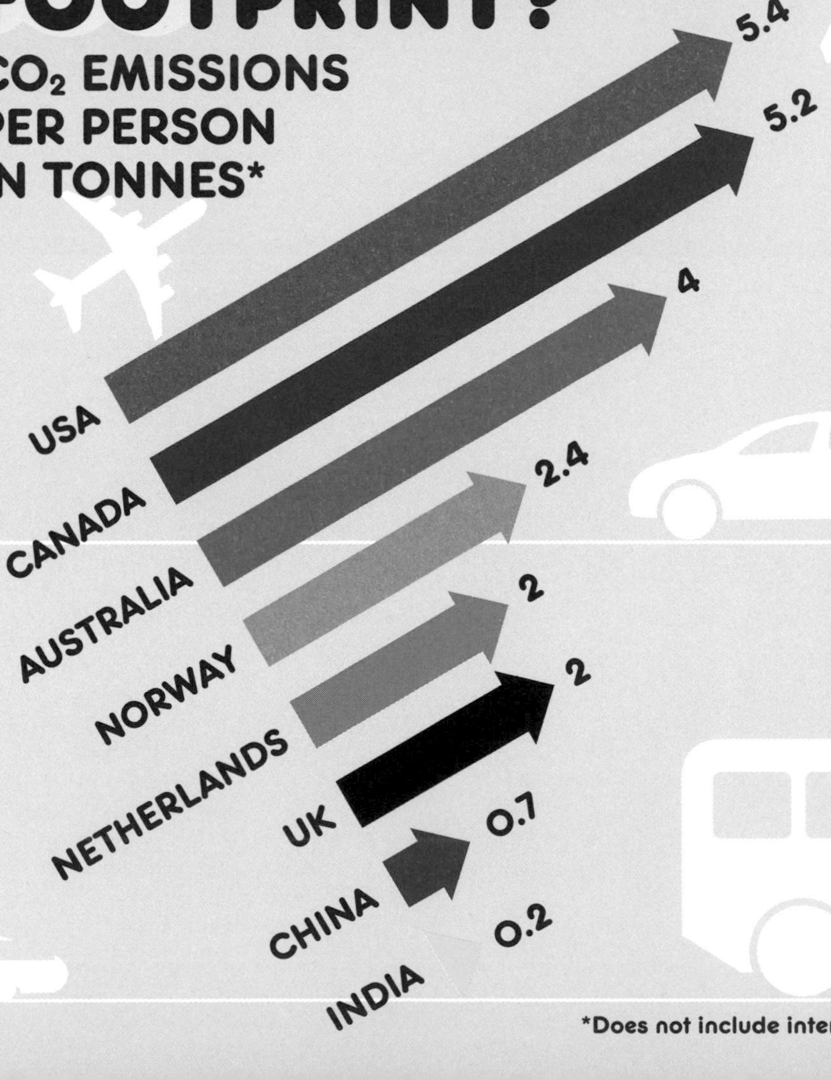

USA — 5.4

CANADA — 5.2

AUSTRALIA — 4

NORWAY — 2.4

NETHERLANDS — 2

UK — 2

CHINA — 0.7

INDIA — 0.2

*Does not include international air travel

WHO USES THE MOST ELECTRIC PASSENGER VEHICLES?

NUMBER OF CARS PER 1,000 PEOPLE

NORWAY
81

ICELAND
37

SWEDEN
21

NETHERLANDS
11

GERMANY
9

FRANCE
7

UK
7

USA
5

WHAT'S THE COST OF YOUR FAVOURITE FAST FOOD?

1. CHOOSE A MAIN

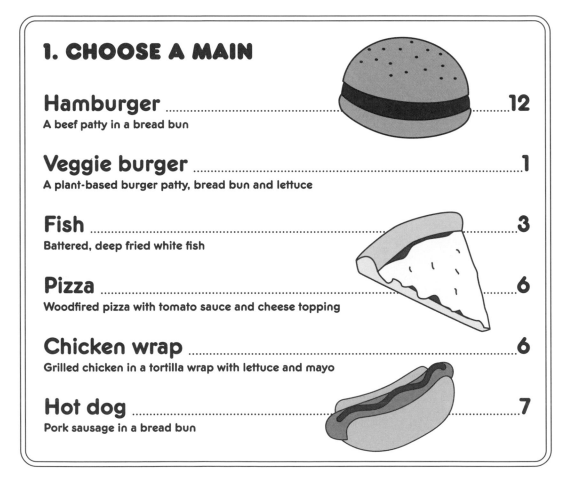

Hamburger 12
A beef patty in a bread bun

Veggie burger 1
A plant-based burger patty, bread bun and lettuce

Fish 3
Battered, deep fried white fish

Pizza 6
Woodfired pizza with tomato sauce and cheese topping

Chicken wrap 6
Grilled chicken in a tortilla wrap with lettuce and mayo

Hot dog 7
Pork sausage in a bread bun

2. ANY EXTRAS?

Extra beef patty............11

Cheese 4

Fries 3

Cheesy fries 6

Salad 1

Bacon / ham 3

3. EAT IN OR TAKE AWAY?

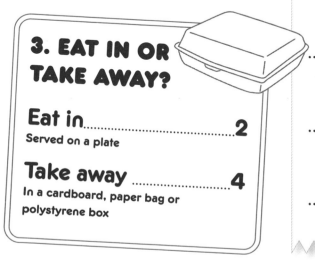

Eat in...........................2
Served on a plate

Take away 4
In a cardboard, paper bag or
polystyrene box

WHAT'S THE COST?

Over 35 – Really bad
CO_2 emissions – over 6.5kg

25-35 – Very bad
CO_2 emissions – 5–6.5kg

15-25 – Not great
CO_2 emissions – 2.5–5kg

10-15 – Not too bad
CO_2 emissions – 1.5–2.5kg

Under 10 – Good
CO_2 emissions – 0.2–1kg

FARMING ANIMALS NEEDS A LOT OF SPACE

THE SPACE NEEDED FOR MEAT, DAIRY, GRAZING AND GROWING CROPS TO FEED THE ANIMALS TAKES UP 27% OF ALL THE WORLD'S LAND

THE SAME AS THIS

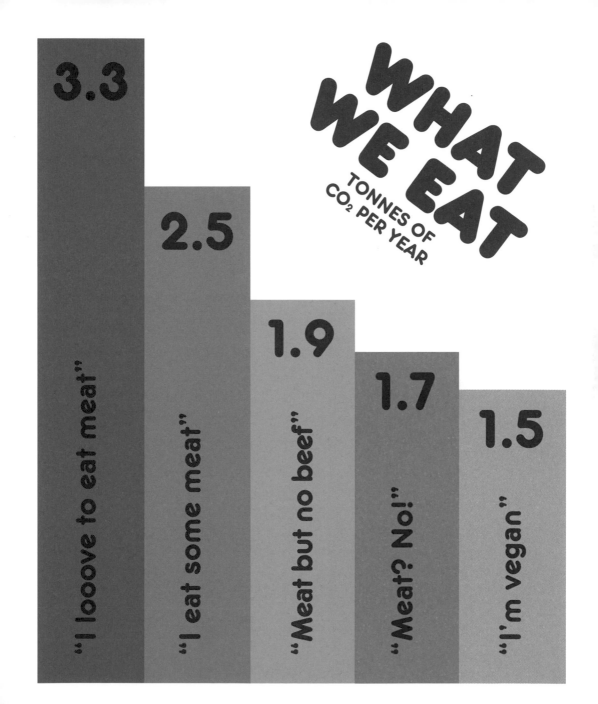

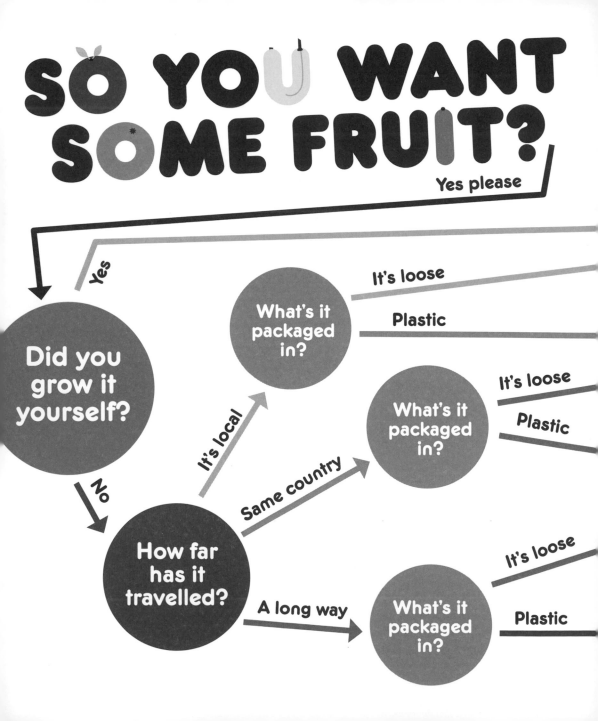

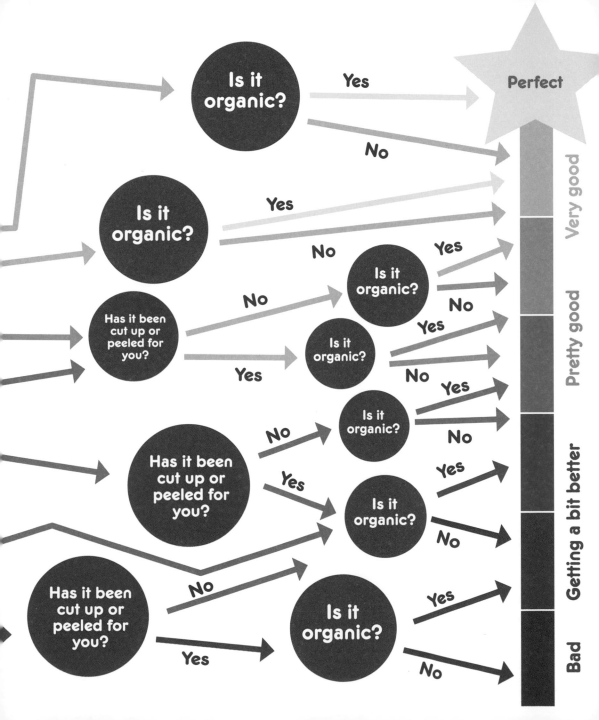

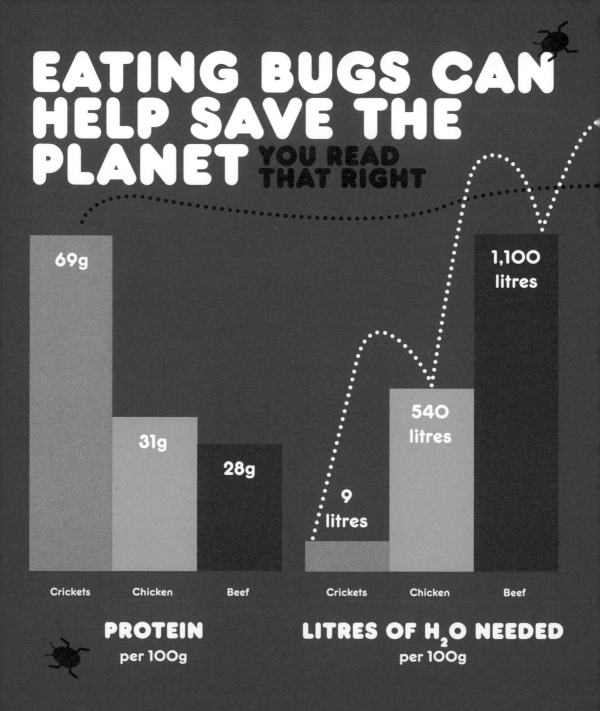

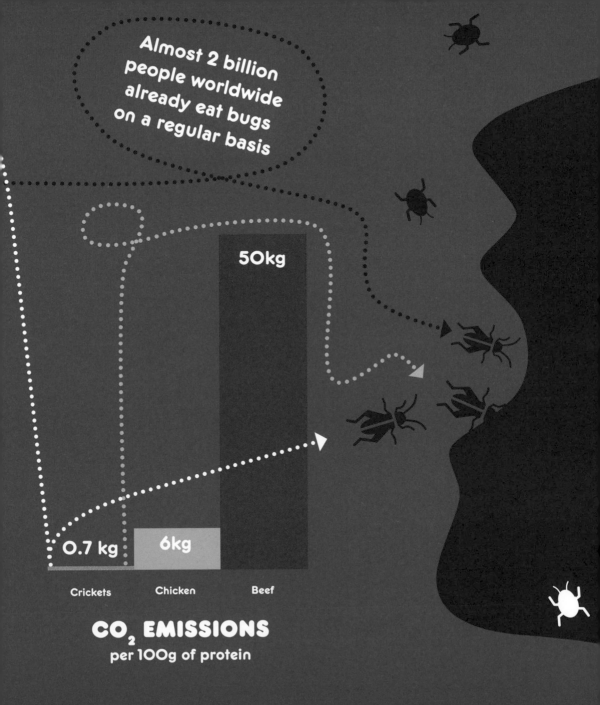

EAT WHAT YOU BUY
BUY WHAT YOU EAT

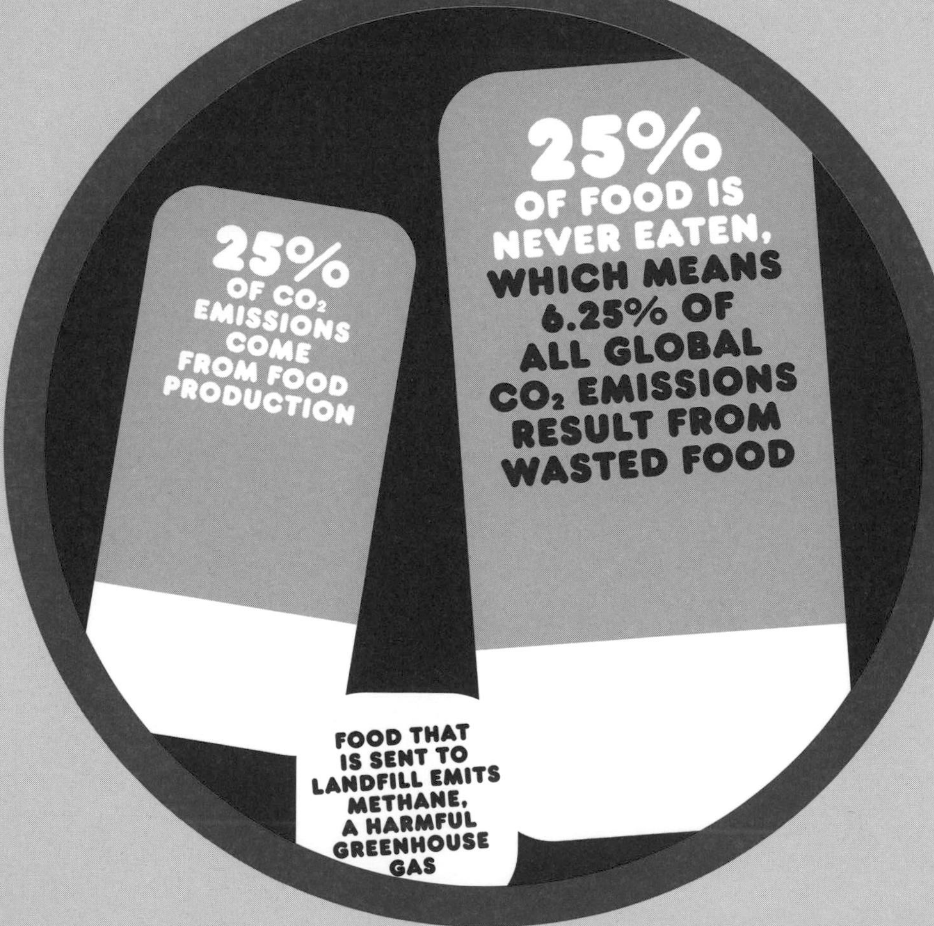

WHAT FOOD DO WE WASTE MOST OF?

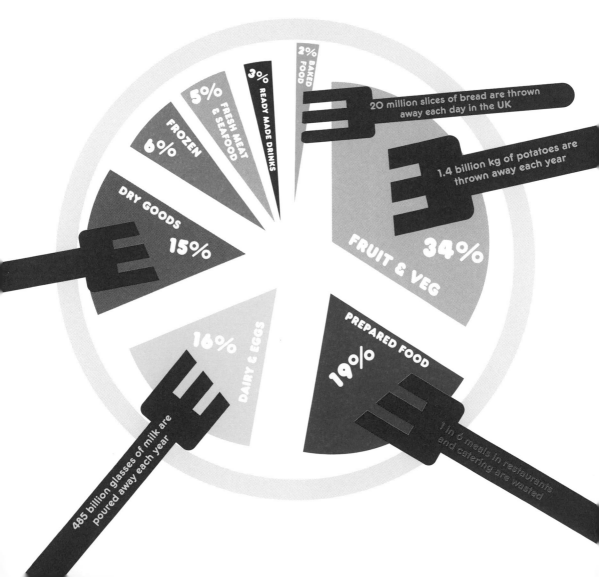

2% BAKED FOOD

3% READY MADE DRINKS

5% FRESH MEAT & SEAFOOD

6% FROZEN

DRY GOODS 15%

16% DAIRY & EGGS

34% FRUIT & VEG

PREPARED FOOD 19%

20 million slices of bread are thrown away each day in the UK

1.4 billion kg of potatoes are thrown away each year

485 billion glasses of milk are poured away each year

1 in 6 meals in restaurants and catering are wasted

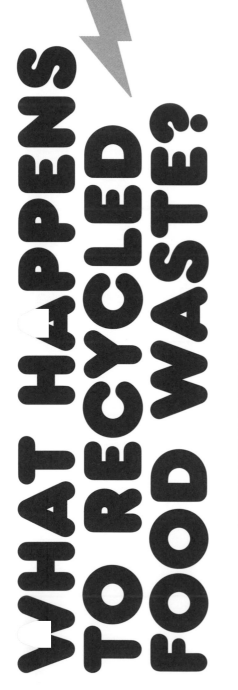

WHAT HAPPENS TO RECYCLED FOOD WASTE?

FOOD WASTE IS PUT INTO A TANK
OXYGEN IS REMOVED

MICROORGANISMS BREAK THE FOOD DOWN
BIOGAS IS RELEASED

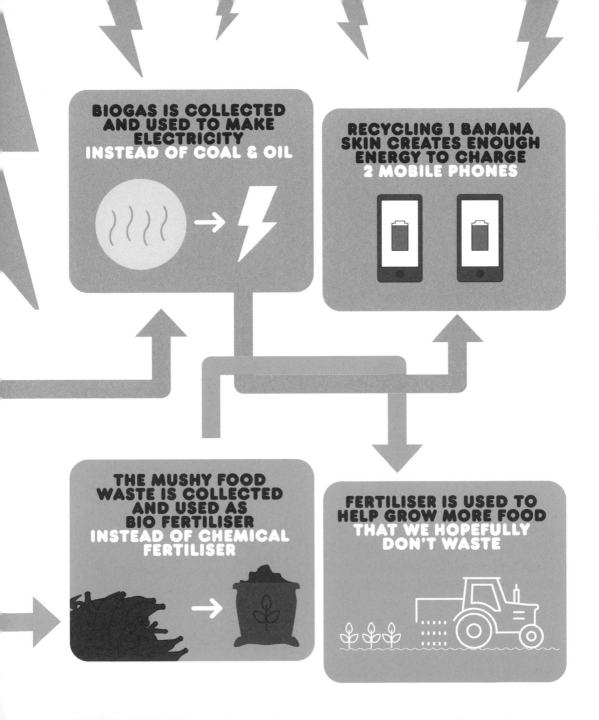

TH- ENVIRONM-NTAL COST OF THE CLOTHES WE WEAR

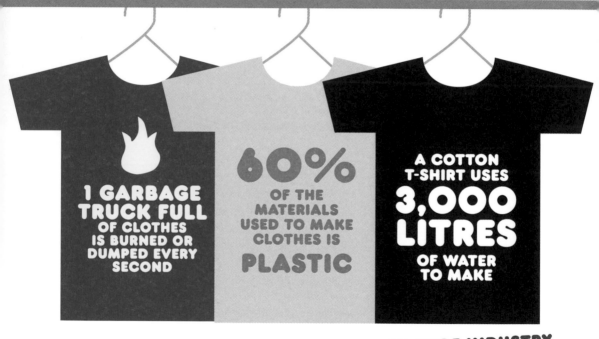

1 GARBAGE TRUCK FULL OF CLOTHES IS BURNED OR DUMPED EVERY SECOND

60% OF THE MATERIALS USED TO MAKE CLOTHES IS **PLASTIC**

A COTTON T-SHIRT USES **3,000 LITRES** OF WATER TO MAKE

300,000,000 SHOES ARE THROWN AWAY EACH YEAR

THE SPORTS SHOE INDUSTRY GENERATES THE SAME AMOUNT OF CO_2 EVERY YEAR AS **66,000,000 CARS**

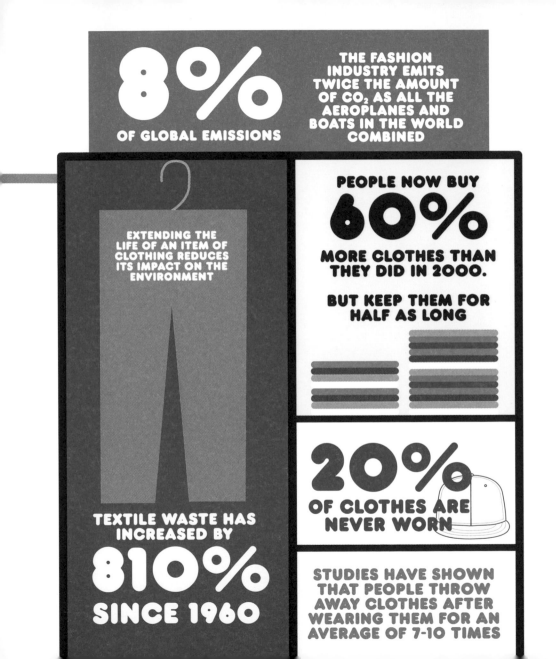

8%
OF GLOBAL EMISSIONS

THE FASHION INDUSTRY EMITS TWICE THE AMOUNT OF CO_2 AS ALL THE AEROPLANES AND BOATS IN THE WORLD COMBINED

EXTENDING THE LIFE OF AN ITEM OF CLOTHING REDUCES ITS IMPACT ON THE ENVIRONMENT

PEOPLE NOW BUY **60%** MORE CLOTHES THAN THEY DID IN 2000.

BUT KEEP THEM FOR HALF AS LONG

20% OF CLOTHES ARE NEVER WORN

TEXTILE WASTE HAS INCREASED BY **810%** SINCE 1960

STUDIES HAVE SHOWN THAT PEOPLE THROW AWAY CLOTHES AFTER WEARING THEM FOR AN AVERAGE OF 7-10 TIMES

GLOBAL E-WASTE

Electronic products that are unwanted, not working, or nearing or at the end of their useful life

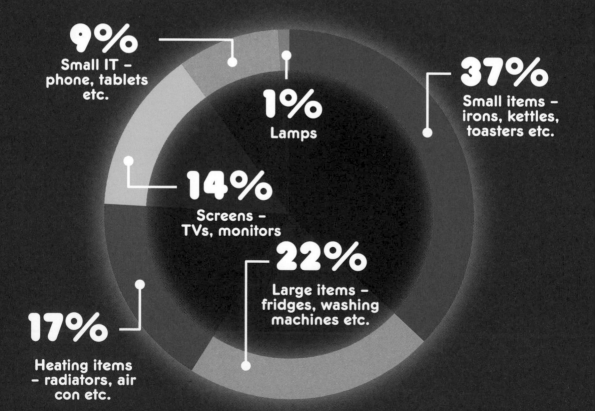

9%
Small IT –
phone, tablets
etc.

1%
Lamps

37%
Small items –
irons, kettles,
toasters etc.

14%
Screens –
TVs, monitors

22%
Large items –
fridges, washing
machines etc.

17%
Heating items
– radiators, air
con etc.

ELECTRONIC WASTE

Millions of tonnes of E-waste per year, projected based on the current rate of growth

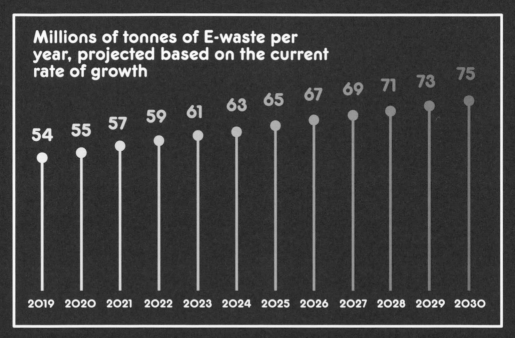

54 2019
55 2020
57 2021
59 2022
61 2023
63 2024
65 2025
67 2026
69 2027
71 2028
73 2029
75 2030

17% E-waste recycled

83% E-waste not recycled

Toxic elements that are not disposed of properly leak into the ground

Lead
Arsenic
Beryllium
Antimony

IF YOU CAN'T REDUCE AND YOU CAN'T REUSE, THEN RECYCLE

5%
OF EARTH'S POPULATION

PRODUCE OVER 40%
OF EARTH'S WASTE

RECYCLING 1 PLASTIC BOTTLE SAVES ENOUGH ENERGY TO POWER A LIGHT BULB FOR 6 HOURS

ALUMINIUM IS EASY TO RECYCLE AND CAN BE RECYCLED INFINITELY. IN THE UK

69%

IS RECYCLED

GLASS CAN ALSO BE RECYCLED INFINITE TIMES

WHILST CHINA RECYCLES

99.5%

OF THEIR ALUMINIUM WASTE

17%

OF THE WASTE PRODUCED BY THE UK IS RECYCLED (NOT A LOT)

1 TONNE OF PAPER RECYCLED SAVES

17 TREES

IF THE UK RECYCLED 10% MORE PAPER IT WOULD SAVE 5 MILLION TREES A YEAR

RECYCLING CARDBOARD SAVES

25%

OF THE ENERGY REQUIRED TO MAKE NEW CARDBOARD

UP TO 60% OF THE WASTE THAT ENDS UP IN THE BIN COULD BE RECYCLED

ONLY 47%
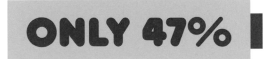

OF BATTERIES ARE RECYCLED. BATTERIES CONTAIN DANGEROUS CHEMICALS INCLUDING LEAD, CADMIUM, ZINC, LITHIUM AND MERCURY

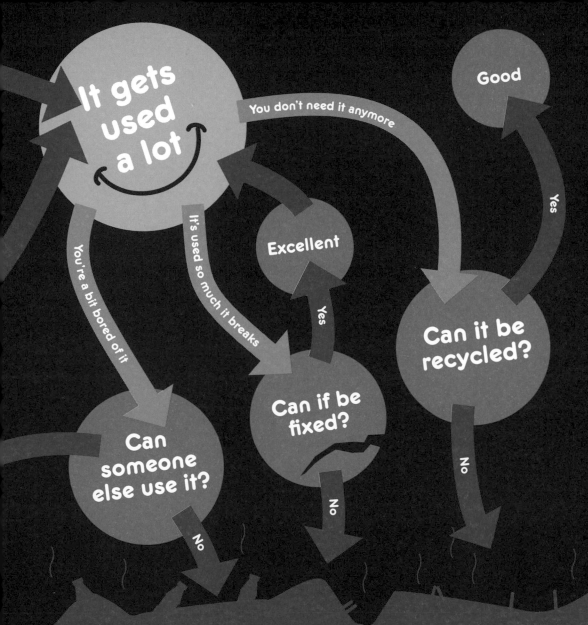

If we don't reduce, reuse or recycle, things end up in landfill, leaching into the soil and releasing emissions

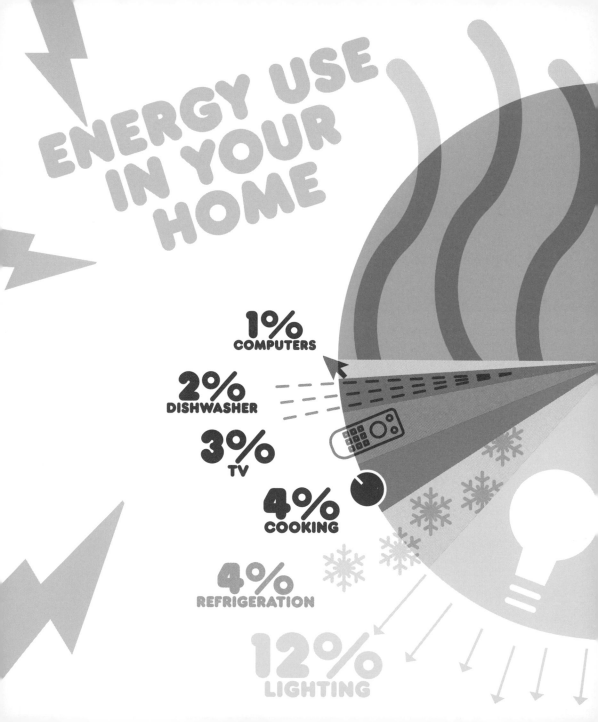

ENERGY USE IN YOUR HOME

1% COMPUTERS

2% DISHWASHER

3% TV

4% COOKING

4% REFRIGERATION

12% LIGHTING

47%
HEATING AND COOLING

14%
WATER HEATING

13%
WASHER / DRYER

WE'VE KNOWN ABOUT THIS FOR A LONG TIME

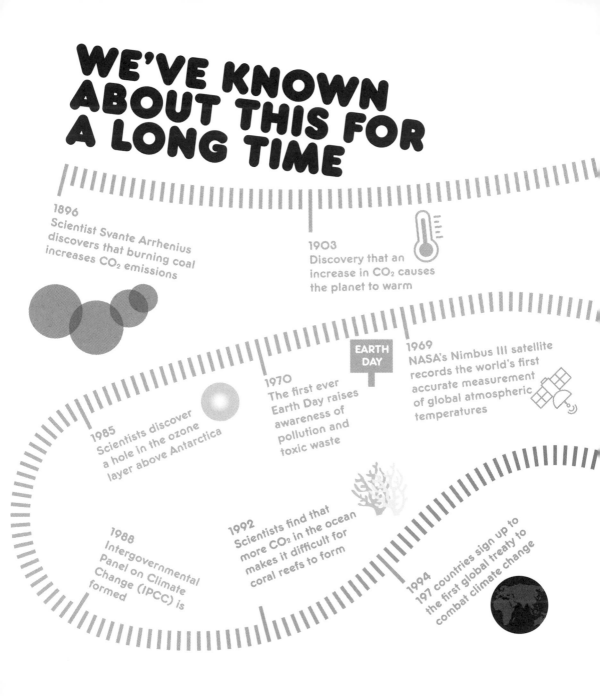

1896
Scientist Svante Arrhenius discovers that burning coal increases CO_2 emissions

1903
Discovery that an increase in CO_2 causes the planet to warm

1969
NASA's Nimbus III satellite records the world's first accurate measurement of global atmospheric temperatures

EARTH DAY

1970
The first ever Earth Day raises awareness of pollution and toxic waste

1985
Scientists discover a hole in the ozone layer above Antarctica

1988
Intergovernmental Panel on Climate Change (IPCC) is formed

1992
Scientists find that more CO_2 in the ocean makes it difficult for coral reefs to form

1994
197 countries sign up to the first global treaty to combat climate change

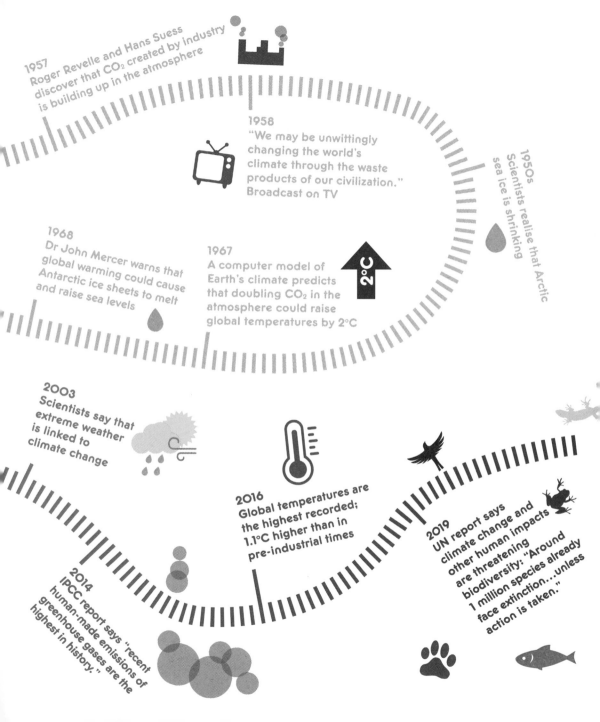

1957
Roger Revelle and Hans Suess discover that CO_2 created by industry is building up in the atmosphere

1958
"We may be unwittingly changing the world's climate through the waste products of our civilization."
Broadcast on TV

1950s
Scientists realise that Arctic sea ice is shrinking

1968
Dr John Mercer warns that global warming could cause Antarctic ice sheets to melt and raise sea levels

1967
A computer model of Earth's climate predicts that doubling CO_2 in the atmosphere could raise global temperatures by 2°C

2°C

2003
Scientists say that extreme weather is linked to climate change

2016
Global temperatures are the highest recorded; 1.1°C higher than in pre-industrial times

2019
UN report says climate change and other human impacts are threatening biodiversity: "Around 1 million species already face extinction...unless action is taken."

2014
IPCC report says "recent human-made emissions of greenhouse gases are the highest in history."

QUITE BIG THINGS YOU CAN DO TO REDUCE YOUR CARBON EMISSIONS

TONNES OF CO$_2$ EMISSIONS YOU COULD SAVE PER YEAR

0.7

0.5

0.5

Eat a vegetarian diet

0.2

0.2

Recycle

Don't use tumble dryer

Replace your petrol car with a hybrid

5 less items of clothing a year

2.4

Live car-free

1.7

1 less long-haul return flight

1.5

Change to an electric car

1.3

Use renewable electricity

0.8

Eat a vegan diet

We don't need a handful of people doing zero waste perfectly. We need millions of people doing it imperfectly.

Anne-Marie Bonneau,
Zero Waste Chef

SMALL THINGS YOU CAN DO AROUND YOUR HOME TO MAKE A BIG DIFFERENCE

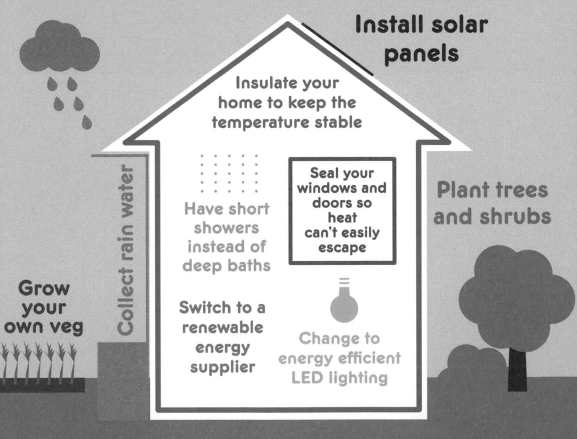

Install solar panels

Insulate your home to keep the temperature stable

Collect rain water

Have short showers instead of deep baths

Seal your windows and doors so heat can't easily escape

Plant trees and shrubs

Grow your own veg

Switch to a renewable energy supplier

Change to energy efficient LED lighting

Let your lawn grow wild

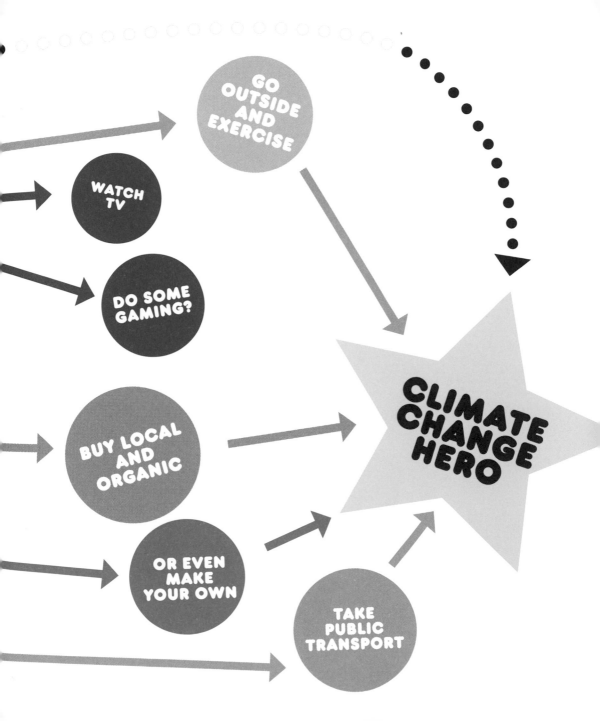

While putting this book together, I've encountered many differing opinions and varying statistics. Numbers can often be interpreted in different ways, and sometimes even the most reliable resources contradict themselves and each other.

I've tried to keep an open mind about everything I've read or looked at, and asked myself questions like:

How expert are the authors or researchers?

How recent is the information?

Do articles have trustworthy sources?

Does the article sound too angry?!

So thanks to those who do the hard work and make this information available. And thanks to Ziggy at Cicada Books for asking me to make the book and helping along the way. I've learnt more than I thought there was to learn and changed many lazy habits that I hope will make a difference.

And thanks for looking at it. I hope it makes a difference to you as well.

Changing World

Sources include: climate.gov, Intergovernmental Panel on Climate Change (IPCC), Met Office, NASA, ourworlddata.org, United Nations, WWF

Text and illustration © David Gibson

British Library Cataloguing-in-Publication Data.

A CIP record for this book is available from the British Library
ISBN: 978-1-80066-028-1

First published in 2022 in the UK, 2023 in the USA

Cicada Books Ltd
48 Burghley Road
London, NW5 1UE
www.cicadabooks.co.uk

Printed in Poland on FSC ® certified paper

MIX
Paper from responsible sources
FSC® C163799